2295

A Tohono O'odham Grammar

A Tohono O'odham Grammar

Ofelia Zepeda

The University of Arizona Press
Tucson

Since the publication of this edition in 1983, the Papago Indian Tribe has officially changed its name to Tohono O'odham (Desert People). This change became effective with the adoption of the new constitution in January 1986 by members of the Tohono O'odham Nation.

The University of Arizona Press
© 1983 The Arizona Board of Regents
All rights reserved

Library of Congress Cataloging-in-Publication Data
Zepeda, Ofelia
A Papago grammar.
Includes index.
1. Papago language—Grammar. I. Title.
PM2123.Z28 1982 497'.4 82-17389
ISBN 0-8165-0792-9

Manufactured in the United States of America on acid-free, archival-quality paper containing a minimum of 50% post-consumer waste and processed chlorine free.

12 11 10 09 08 07 10 9 8 7 6 5

To the Tohono 'O'odham
and to my father, Albert
and the memory of Juliana Zepeda

Contents

Introduction

The Papago people—or, as they call themselves, the 'O'odham—reside in southern Arizona and northern Mexico, where they have lived for centuries. Most of the 'O'odham live on four reservations in southern Arizona. The main reservation, with its Indian agency at Sells, covers the largest area. The other three, much smaller, reservations are San Xavier (or Wa:k) near Tucson (Cuk Ṣon), 'Akĭ Ciñ near Phoenix, and the Gila Bend reservation in southwestern Arizona. Not all of the 'O'odham live on the reservations; many live in towns near them—such as Ajo, Maricopa, and Casa Grande—as well as in the cities of Phoenix and Tucson.

Covering more than two and a half million acres, the main Papago Indian reservation is the second largest (after the Navajo) in the United States. Since there are approximately twelve thousand Papagos,* the population density relative to the land area is small; however, the Papagos actually constitute a relatively large tribal population as compared to other American Indians.

The Papago Language

The tribal language of the Papagos is a member of the American Indian language family known as Uto-Aztecan. One of the largest of these language families in terms of both number of languages and geographical area, Uto-Aztecan comprises some two dozen extant languages, some spoken as far north as southern Idaho and some as far south as southern Mexico. Uto-Aztecan is generally divided into eight subfamilies. The Papago language belongs to the subfamily called Tepiman (or sometimes Pimic). This subfamily includes—in addition to Papago—Pima, Tepecano, and Tepehuan.

As of early 1983, no investigations have been carried out to determine how many Papagos still speak the language. Perhaps this is a good sign, since these studies are usually initiated only if the language is presumed or known to be dying. According to school district officials in Sells, the best estimate as to the number of Papagos

*According to U.S. Census figures, 1980.

who still speak Papago fluently in the early 1980s is more than two-thirds of the population, or approximately seventy to seventy-five percent. This relatively high percentage may be due to the fact that many Papago villages are still fairly isolated and are uncontaminated by outside influences. However, this situation has begun to change. Many of the people who once lived in isolated or semi-isolated villages have started to move to more populous areas, such as Sells, the largest community on the main Papago reservation. The migration has been due to various factors, including economic and social ones, and its result has been to introduce many Papagos into a society dominated by English. Thus, many young Papagos appear to be less fluent in Papago than their elders; many say they speak only a little, others that they don't speak Papago at all, but understand it. It is my hope that this pedagogical grammar will allow these Papagos to learn and appreciate their native language.

Organization of the Book

The material in this text has been tested and refined in actual classroom application and has gone through a number of revisions in form and content based on this practical experience. The book provides extensive coverage of the structure of Papago, beginning with the most basic elements and concluding with the more complex. The book is intended for classroom use in teaching native and non-native speakers in junior high, high school, and college. Although there are some differences between Papago and Pima, teachers who have used this grammar have found it quite adequate for teaching Pimas the basics about their language. The book is also useful for linguists who want an overview of the structure of the Papago language, although the lessons are designed to be understood by students with little or no background in either linguistics or Papago.

As a pedagogical grammar, the book is divided into four parts. Parts I and II are grammar units of ten lessons and one review lesson each. Part III consists of five Papago dialogs, and Part IV comprises several types of supplementary material: a list of abbreviations and symbols, a summary of grammatical elements, two glossaries, and the index.

Each individual lesson in the grammar units begins with a vocabulary section, followed by explanations of specific grammar points. In addition to text, the explanatory section includes sample sentences, grammar notes, and grammar rules. The lesson then concludes with a section of practical exercises designed to reinforce the student's comprehension.

Research on the structure of the language was an ongoing project at the time of the publication of this first book on Papago grammar. Consequently, certain points still awaited thorough linguistic analysis.

The Writing System

The writing system used in this grammar, based on internationally recognized linguistic symbols, was developed by Albert Alvarez and Kenneth Hale in the late 1960s. Chosen as the official orthographic system of the Papago tribe in 1974, this is the system taught in schools which deal with bilingual-bicultural education both on and off the reservation. There are some differences between the Alvarez/Hale orthography and the system devised for the *Papago and Pima to English Dictionary* by Dean and Lucille Saxton (University of Arizona Press), but the two systems are similar in most respects. The differences, which affect only vowel length and six consonants, are so slight that both systems are easily understood and adapted by Papago students.

The Pima language has its own writing system, but it, too, is very similar to the one used in this grammar, so that Pima speakers need to make only a few small orthographic adaptations. A precise, detailed comparison between the Alvarez/Hale system and the Saxton system is presented in the first lesson on the sounds of Papago (see page 5).

Language Tape

A pronunciation guide, which gives approximate English equivalents for Papago sounds, is provided in the first lesson of this grammar (see page 4). In addition, a language tape, recorded by a native speaker, has been prepared to accompany the text. Readers who wish to obtain a copy of this tape should contact Ofelia Zepeda, c/o Department of Linguistics, University of Arizona, Tucson, Arizona 85721.

Acknowledgments

I am honored to express my gratitude to the people who have helped me in my work on the Papago language, in developing my linguistic expertise, and in the preparation and revision of this book. I wish to thank Dean and Lucille Saxton for their contributions to the linguistic materials available on both Papago and Pima. It is from these materials that many Papagos (including myself) and Pimas first became acquainted with the written form of our languages. Dr. Dan Matson taught me how to read and write Papago, gave me my first exposure to the structure of the Papago language, and provided me with a secure foundation from which to expand. Dr. Kenneth Hale —my teacher, my friend, and, sometimes, my student—began the work which led to these lessons. He reintroduced me to my native language, strengthened my knowledge of its structure, and taught me the principles of linguistic analysis. Dr. Adrian Akmajian's expertise in syntax as well as his writing and organizational skills were invaluable in the restructuring of the material into a more cogent set of lessons. His suggestions led to the addition of more grammatical description and explanation, as well as some translations that had simply been taken for granted. Dr. Susan Steele worked with me on Papago morphology and helped me to express in English some of the ideas I had about Papago. With her expert advice and encouragement, a final revision of all the Papago material from beginning to end was completed.

I thank the many Papago speakers who contributed to this grammar by providing me with example sentences and ideas for dialogs and by trying out the exercises to see if they made sense. I also acknowledge Theresa Huard-Lentz and Lin Hall for their typing of the manuscript.

Finally, I am most grateful to the National Endowment for the Humanities for support of the project that led to this book and to the University of Arizona Press for bringing about its publication.

OFELIA ZEPEDA

PART I
First Grammar Unit

LESSON 1

The Sounds of Papago

PRONUNCIATION GUIDE

Before reviewing the pronunciation guide shown below, there are two important elements of the Papago language that must be recognized: the *location of stress within a word* and the *glottal stop.* The stress on Papago words is consistently in initial position—that is, on the first syllable. The glottal stop (') is a sound produced by a stoppage of air in the throat and is also found in certain expressions in American English. For example, most English speakers have a glottal stop in the middle of the expression *"oh-oh"* (as in *"Oh-oh, I think we're in trouble!"*). Many speakers of English also pronounce the word *button* with a glottal stop sound, rather than a *t* sound, in the middle of the word.

Listed on the next page are the spelling symbols used in this grammar (based on the Alvarez/Hale system) and their approximate English equivalent sounds.

Another important point is that the sound of each of the Papago vowels can be drawn out to a long sound or cut off as a short sound. The sound of a long or short vowel does not change—it is simply held for a longer or shorter duration. The long vowels in this grammar are marked by a colon following the letter (e.g., **ma:gina, we:nag, wi:b, ko:ṣ, hu:ñ**). Short vowels are represented by a breve (˘) over the letter (e.g., **dahă, hehĕ, 'uwĭ, wo:po'ŏ**). The long vowels can appear in any syllable of a word; short vowels, which are almost whispered by most Papago speakers, usually occur at the end of a word.

SPELLING SYMBOL (ALVAREZ/HALE SYSTEM)	APPROXIMATE ENGLISH EQUIVALENT
a	like the *a* in *father*
b	like the *b* in *big*
c	like the *ch* in *chip*
d	like the *th* in *this*
ḍ	like the *t* with a glottal stop in *but*
e	like the *u* in *hum*
g	like the *g* in *go*
h	like the *h* in *hat*
i	like the *i* in *machine*
j	like the *j* in *job*
k	like the *k* in *kiss*
l	(no similar sound in English—the closest is the *dd* in *ladder;* also similar to the single *r* in Spanish)
m	like the *m* in *miss*
n	like the *n* in *no*
ñ	like the *ny* in *canyon*
ŋ	like the *ng* in *finger*
o	like the *a* in *all*
p	like the *p* in *pot*
s	like the *s* in *see*
ṣ	like the *sh* in *ship*
t	like the *t* in *top*
u	like the *u* in *brute*
w	like the *w* in *win*
y	like the *y* in *yes*

When two vowels occur together in a Papago word, the resulting diphthongs (the second vowel is always "i") can produce new sounds, as listed below:

PAPAGO DIPHTHONG	APPROXIMATE ENGLISH EQUIVALENT
ai	like the *i* in *bite*
ei	(no similar sound in English—run the two separate sounds of the Papago *e* and *i* together to make one sound)
oi	like the *oy* in *boy*
ui	like the *ooey* in *gooey*

ORTHOGRAPHIC SYSTEMS: A COMPARISON

The writing system used in this grammar, based on international linguistic symbols, was developed in the late 1960s by Albert Alvarez and Kenneth Hale. Recognized as the official orthographic system of the Papago tribe in 1974, it has been used since then in schools that teach Papago and other language arts classes both on and off the reservation. The system designed for the *Papago and Pima to English Dictionary* by Dean and Lucille Saxton (University of Arizona Press) is quite similar to this system, and the two are reciprocally adaptable. The orthographic adaptations to be made, which affect only vowel length and six consonants, are listed below:

ALVAREZ/HALE SYSTEM		SAXTON SYSTEM	
Long Vowel	*Sample Word*	*Long Vowel*	*Sample Word*
a:	ma:gina	ah	mahgina
e:	we:nag	eh	wehnag
i:	wi:b	ih	wihb
o:	'o:'o	oh	oh'o
u:	'u:s	uh	uhs
Short Vowel	*Sample Word*	*Short Vowel*	*Sample Word*
ă	dahă	Not treated orthographically; a discussion on the occurrences of these vowels is in an appendix of the dictionary.	
ĕ	hehĕ		
ĭ	'uwĭ		
ŏ	wo:po'ŏ		
Consonant	*Sample Word*	*Consonant*	*Sample Word*
c	cucul	ch	chuchul
d	da:k	th*	thahk
ḍ	meḍ	d*	med
ñ	ñe'e	(Not treated orthographically; discussion in an appendix of dictionary.)	
ŋ	ca:ŋgo	ng	chahngo
ṣ	ṣu:ṣk	sh	shuhshk

Note that initial glottal stops are not represented orthographically in the Saxton system but are present in the Alvarez/Hale system.

*In the 1969 edition *th* was written *d* and *d* was written *D.*

The writing system for the Pima language is also very similar to the one used in this grammar. In fact, there are only two orthographic differences: Pima uses *ch* for *c* and *sh* for *s.* All other letters and symbols correspond to the Alvarez/Hale system. The major difference between the two languages is that where Papago uses a *w,* Pima has a *v;* however, this orthographic change reflects an actual difference in pronunciation.

LESSON 2

Intransitive Sentences

VOCABULARY

NOUNS

Singular	*Plural*
'ali child, baby	**'a'al** children, babies
cehia young girl, girl	**cecia** young girls, girls
ceoj man, boy	**cecoj** men, boys
'O'odham* Papago person	**'O'odham** Papago persons
'uwĭ woman, girl	**'u'uwĭ** women, girls

VERBS†

cicwi playing	**cicwi** playing
cipkan working	**cicpkan** working
ñeok speaking	**ñeñok** speaking
ṣoak crying	**ṣoañ** crying

OTHER EXPRESSIONS

hegai that	**hegam** those
'i:da this	**'idam** these
'o is/was	**'o** are/were
pi not (*negative marker*)	—

*Used in lower case, **'o'odham** refers simply to any person or any human being.

†All verbs in the vocabulary sections of each chapter are given in the imperfective (progressive) form unless otherwise noted.

NOTE: The simplest way that plural forms (for both nouns and verbs) are created in Papago is by *reduplication:* the first consonant and vowel or just the initial vowel is repeated. Thus, **gogs** (dog) becomes **gogogs** (dogs) and **'ali** (child) becomes **'a'al** (children). There are, however, several other processes by which a plural form can be created; these processes are extremely complex and not yet fully understood. The plural forms in this teaching grammar will, therefore, be learned simply as additional vocabulary items.

SIMPLE INTRANSITIVE SENTENCES

The following examples illustrate simple intransitive sentences in Papago:

1. **'I:da 'o'odham 'o ñeok.** This person is/was speaking.
2. **Hegai 'uwǐ 'o cipkan.** That woman is/was working.

The word **'o** in these sentences is the imperfective form of the Papago auxiliary or, for short, *aux.* All sentences in Papago have an aux. The aux **'o** indicates *ongoing action* in the *present* or *past.* A simple intransitive sentence has a subject, an aux, and a verb.

The first important thing to know about Papago is the position of the aux. The sentences in (1) and (2) can also be said as in (3) and (4).

3. **Ñeok 'o 'i:da 'o'odham.** This person is/was speaking.
4. **Cipkan 'o hegai 'uwǐ.** That woman is/was working.

The meaning of (1) is the same as the meaning of (3) and the meaning of (2) is the same as the meaning of (4). The only difference between (1) and (3) or between (2) and (4) is the word order. In (1) and (2) the subject is at the beginning of the sentence and the verb is at the end; in (3) and (4) the subject is at the end of the sentence, while the verb is at the beginning. That is, (1) and (2) have the order:

SUBJECT AUX VERB

But (3) and (4) have the order:

VERB AUX SUBJECT

However, it is impossible for the aux **'o** to move around in a sentence.

In all four sentences above, the aux is in *second position* and it cannot move around to other places in the sentence, unlike the subject and the verb. Thus, one of the first rules of the Papago language is the following:

Rule 1: The aux occurs in second position in a sentence.

NOTE: In the example **Hegai 'uwǐ 'o cipkan** (That woman is/was working), it appears that the aux **'o** is in third position, contrary to Rule I, which states that the aux is always in second position.

However, Rule I still holds, since the determiner **hegai** (that) and the noun **'uwĭ** (woman) are taken as a whole and, thus, count as one position. It should also be noted that a noun and its determiner are moved together as a single item when the word order in a sentence is changed.

NEGATIVE INTRANSITIVE SENTENCES

The negative in Papago is **pi.** Examples (5) and (6) illustrate a negative form of the sentences in (1) and (2).

5. **'I:da 'o'odham 'o pi ñeok.** This person is/was not speaking.
   SUBJECT AUX NEG VERB

6. **Hegai 'uwĭ 'o pi cipkan.** This woman is/was not working.
   SUBJECT AUX NEG VERB

Note that the auxiliary is second and the negative follows it. In sentences in which the negative follows the auxiliary, the verb cannot occur at the front of the sentence. Thus, the following is a bad (*) sentence:

7. ***Ñeok 'o pi 'i:da 'o'odham.**
   VERB AUX NEG SUBJECT

The negative does not have to follow the auxiliary. The negative can precede the auxiliary, but when it does nothing else does, because the *auxiliary must be in second position.* Examples (8) and (9) are like (5) and (6), but the negative is at the beginning of the sentence.

8. **Pi 'o ñeok 'i:da 'o'odham.** This person is/was not speaking.
   NEG AUX VERB SUBJECT

9. **Pi 'o cipkan hegai 'uwĭ.** That woman is/was not working.
   NEG AUX VERB SUBJECT

The following are more examples of negative sentences:

10. a. **'I:da 'ali 'o pi ṣoak.**
    b. **Pi 'o ṣoak 'i:da 'ali.**
    } This baby is/was not crying.

11. a. **Hegai cehia 'o pi cicwi.**
    b. **Pi 'o cicwi hegai cehia.**
    } That girl is/was not playing.

IMPERFECTIVE VERBS: SINGULAR AND PLURAL FORMS

All the sentences above have been in the singular. In intransitive Papago sentences when the subject is singular, so is the verb, and when the subject is plural, so is the verb. (Transitive sentences, which follow a different rule, are explained in Lesson 6.) The following sentences illustrate the use of plural forms in intransitive sentences:

12. a. **Hegam 'O'odham 'o cicpkan.** b. **Cicpkan 'o hegam 'O'odham.**	Those Papago persons are/were working.
13. a. **'Idam cecoj 'o ñeñok.** b. **Ñeñok 'o 'idam cecoj.**	These boys are/were speaking.
14. a. **Hegam 'u'uwǐ 'o pi cickpan.** b. **Pi 'o cicpkan hegam 'u'uwǐ.**	Those women are/were not working.
15. a. **'Idam cecoj 'o pi ñeñok.** b. **Pi 'o ñeñok 'idam cecoj.**	These boys are/were not speaking.
16. a. **Hegam 'a'al 'o pi ṣoañ.** b. **Pi 'o ṣoañ hegam 'a'al.**	Those children are/were not crying.

EXERCISES

A. Translate into English:

1. Ñeñok 'o hegam 'o'odham.
2. 'I:da 'uwǐ 'o cipkan.
3. 'Idam cecia 'o pi cicpkan.
4. Pi 'o ṣoañ hegam 'a'al.
5. Hegai 'ali 'o cicwi.
6. Hegai 'o'odham 'o pi ñeok.
7. Pi 'o ṣoak 'i:da 'ali.
8. Cipkan 'o 'i:da 'uwǐ.

B. Using the vocabulary items below and the rules we have discussed, make up five new sentences in Papago that have not appeared in this lesson. For each new sentence give both possible word orders we have discussed so far.

1. **ke:li** *n.* old man
2. **ñe'ĕ** *v.* sing
3. **'oks** *n.* old lady
4. **hihidoḍ** *v.* cook
5. **je:ñ** *v.* smoking a cigarette
6. **ca:ŋgo** *n.* monkey
7. **mumku** *v.* is sick
8. **ko:ji** *n.* pig
9. **ba:ñimaḍ** *v.* crawl
10. **juḍum** *n.* bear

C. Writing exercise for native speakers. Pick five sentences from this lesson and rewrite each one so that it sounds more natural to you. Discuss how your version is different from the version given in the text.

LESSON 3

The "g" Determiner and *Yes/No* Questions

VOCABULARY

NOUNS

Singular	*Plural*
gogs dog	**gogogs** dogs
haiwañ cow	**hahaiwañ** cows
kawyu horse	**kakawyu** horses
mi:stol cat	**mimstol** cats
ṣu:dagĭ water	—
wisilo calf	**wipsilo** calves

VERBS

him walking	**hihim** walking
hi:nk barking	**hihink** barking
ke:k standing	**gegok** standing
ki: living	**ki:** living
ko:ṣ sleeping	**ko:kṣ** sleeping
meḍ running	**wo:po'ŏ** running

OTHER EXPRESSIONS

'aṣ just
g the, a
ganhu, gnhu over there
heu'u yes
'i:ya right here
pi'a no
ṣa'i actually
si very, really

THE "g" DETERMINER

The following intransitive sentences illustrate again the two word orders discussed in Lesson 2 for simple intransitive sentences:

1. a. **Gogs 'o hi:nk.**
   SUBJECT AUX VERB
   b. **Hi:nk 'o g gogs.**
   VERB AUX DET SUBJECT
   — The dog is/was barking.

2. a. **Kawyu 'o meḍ.**
   SUBJECT AUX VERB
   b. **Meḍ 'o g kawyu.**
   VERB AUX DET SUBJECT
   — The horse is/was running.

However, the (a) and (b) sentences in examples (1) and (2) differ in one important respect. In the (b) sentences, where the subject is at the end of the sentence, the subject is preceded by the word **g,** which is called a determiner (*det,* for short); in the (a) sentences, where the subject is at the beginning of the sentence, there is no **g** determiner preceding the subject. Generally, in Papago, nouns (including names) are preceded by the **g** determiner, but the **g** determiner never occurs at the beginning of a sentence. Thus, we have a second rule for Papago:

> **Rule 2: Always drop the *g* determiner at the beginning of a sentence.**
>
> For example: ***G 'o'odham 'o ñeok** (The person is/was speaking) becomes **'O'odham 'o ñeok.**

The following are more examples of the **g** determiner rule.

3. a. **Haiwañ 'o him.**
   b. **Him 'o g haiwañ.**
   — The cow is/was walking.

4. a. **Mi:stol 'o ko:ṣ.**
   b. **Ko:ṣ 'o g mi:stol.**
   — The cat is/was sleeping.

5. a. **Klisti:na 'o meḍ.**
   b. **Meḍ 'o g Klisti:na.**
   — Christina is/was running.

THE QUESTION MARKER "N"

The following sentences illustrate simple *yes/no* questions in Papago. The term *yes/no question* applies to questions which can be answered with a simple affirmative (e.g., *yes*) or negative (e.g., *no*) answer.

6. a.	**No**	**g**	**mi:stol**	**ko:s?**	Is/was the cat sleeping?
	QUESTION	DET	SUBJECT	VERB	
b.	**No**	**ko:s**	**g**	**mi:ṣtol?**	
	QUESTION	VERB	DET	SUBJECT	
7. a.	**No**	**g**	**gogogs**	**hihink?**	Are/were the dogs barking?
	QUESTION	DET	SUBJECT	VERB	
b.	**No**	**hihink**	**g**	**gogogs?**	
	QUESTION	VERB	DET	SUBJECT	

In creating questions in Papago, the **n–**, or question marker, is placed at the very beginning of the sentence with the auxiliary in second position. Since the auxiliary combines with the **n–**, it loses its initial glottal stop.

Statement: **Hegai kawyu 'o meḍ.**

Question: **N– hegai kawyu 'o meḍ?** *(Auxiliary must be second.)*

Proper Form: **No hegai kawyu meḍ?**

ANSWERING *YES/NO* QUESTIONS

To answer a *yes/no* question, you can simply say **heu'u** (yes) or **pi'a** (no):

Question: **No g 'ali ṣoak?** Is/was the child crying?

Answer: **Heu'u.** Yes. *or:* **Pi'a.** No.

More complete answers are possible. So, if someone asks:

Question: **No g 'ali ṣoak?** Is/was the child crying?

you can answer:

Heu'u, ṣoak 'o g 'ali. Yes, the child is/was crying.

or:

Pi'a, pi 'o ṣoak g 'ali. No, the child is/was not crying.

NOTE: Heu'u and **pi'a** are set off from the rest of the sentence by a comma and are not considered in determining the position of the aux. In answering a question with **pi'a,** the negative particle **pi** must also be included. These answers repeat everything in the question, except for the question particle. It isn't necessary, however, to repeat everything. The sentences below illustrate possible answers to various *yes/no* questions; the parts of the sentences in parentheses are optional.

8. a. **No si hi:nk g gogs?** Is/was the dog really barking?
   b. **Heu'u, si 'o hi:nk (g gogs).** Yes, the dog is/was really barking.
   c. **Pi'a, pi 'o ṣa'i hi:nk (g gogs).** No, the dog is/was not actually barking.

9. a. **No ko:ṣ g mi:stol?** Is/was the cat sleeping?
   b. **Heu'u, ko:ṣ 'o (g mi:stol.)** Yes, the cat is/was sleeping.
   c. **Pi'a, pi 'o ko:ṣ (g mi:stol.)** No, the cat is/was not sleeping.

10. a. **No 'aṣ cicwi g 'a'al?** Are/were the children just playing?
    b. **Heu'u, 'o 'aṣ cicwi (g 'a'al).** Yes, the children are/were just playing.
    c. **Pi'a, pi 'o ṣa'i cicwi (g 'a'al).** No, the children are/were actually not playing.

EXERCISES

A. Change the word order in each of the following sentences, according to the rules we have discussed. Pay attention to the placement of the auxiliary **'o** as well as the **g** determiner.

1. Wo:po'ŏ 'o g gogogs.
2. Ṣoañ 'o 'idam 'o'odham.
3. Mi:stol 'o him.
4. Pi 'o meḍ g 'uwĭ.
5. Haiwañ 'o ko:ṣ.
6. Hegam 'a'al 'o pi cicwi.
7. Hihink 'o g gogogs.
8. Pi 'o ko:kṣ 'idam cecoj.

B. Give a *yes* and *no* answer for each of the following:

Example

No g kawyu meḍ?

a. Heu'u, meḍ 'o (g kawyu).

b. Pi'a, pi 'o meḍ (g kawyu).

1. No g cehia ko:ṣ?
2. No hegam hahaiwañ wo:po'ŏ?
3. No cikpan g 'uwĭ?
4. No cicwi 'idam 'a'al?
5. No g gogs hi:nk?
6. No g wipsilo ṣoañ?
7. No g 'o'odham ñeñok?
8. No wo:po'ŏ g kakawyu?

C. Change each of the following statements into a question.

Examples

Statement: Mimstol 'o ko:kṣ.

Question: No g mimstol ko:kṣ?

Statement: Ko:kṣ 'o g mimstol.

Question: No ko:kṣ g mimstol?

1. 'U'uwĭ 'o cickpan.
2. Ṣoañ 'o g cecia.
3. Hegai ceoj 'o ñeok.
4. Wisilo 'o 'ab him.
5. Hihim 'o g wipsilo.
6. 'Idam kakawyu 'o ko:kṣ.
7. 'A'al 'o cicwi.
8. Ṣoañ 'o hegam 'a'al.

D. For native speakers only. The following sentences illustrate the use of the following vocabulary items from the vocabulary list for this chapter: **'ab, 'am, 'an, 'i:ya, 'amai, ganhu, si,** and **'aṣ.** These small words are frequently used in normal conversational style, and make the sentences more natural sounding than sentences without these particles. For example, sentences (1)–(7) of this lesson do not contain these particles and are not as natural as the corresponding examples below:

1. **Mali:ya 'o 'aṣ ko:ṣ.** Mary is just sleeping.
2. **Ganhu 'o him g wisilo.** The calf is walking over there.
3. **'I:ya 'o ko:kṣ g 'a'al.** The children are sleeping right here.
4. **No 'an meḍ g ṣu:dagĭ?** Is the water running there?
5. **No 'i:ya ki: g Huan?** Does John live here?
6. **'Ab 'o him g Husi.** Joe is coming (toward speaker).
7. **'Am 'o meḍ g Klisti:na.** Christina is running (away from speaker).
8. **'Amai 'o ke:k.** It is standing right there.

Make up an original sentence for each of the particles shown above.

Subject Pronouns and the Imperfective Auxiliary

VOCABULARY

s-ba:bigĭ	slowly
s-hottam	quickly
s-kaidam	loudly
tako	yesterday

INDEPENDENT SUBJECT PRONOUNS

All the sentences we have used in Lessons 2 and 3 have had noun subjects. It is also possible to have an independent pronoun as a subject. The independent pronouns are:

	Singular		*Plural*	
1st person	**'a:ñi**	I	**'a:cim**	we
2nd person	**'a:pi**	you	**'a:pim**	you
3rd person	**hegai**	he, she, it, that	**hegam**	they, those

The following sentences illustrate these independent pronouns used as subjects:

1. a. **'A:ñi 'añ s-ba:bigĭ ñeok.**
   b. **S-ba:bigĭ 'añ ñeok 'a:ñi.**
   } I am/was speaking slowly.

2. a. **'A:pi 'ap s-hottam cipkan.**
   b. **S-hottam 'ap cipkan 'a:pi.**
   } You are/were working quickly.

3. a. **Hegai 'o cicwi.**
   b. **Cicwi 'o hegai.**
   } He (she) is/was playing.

4. a. **'A:cim 'ac ganhu wo:po'ŏ.**
   b. **Ganhu 'ac wo:po'ŏ 'a:cim.**
   } We are/were running over there.

5. a. **'A:pim 'am 'i:ya cicwi.**
   b. **'I:ya 'am cicwi 'a:pim.**
   } You *(pl.)* are/were playing right here.

6. a. **Hegam 'o aṣ ñeñok.**
   b. **'O aṣ ñeñok hegam.**
   } They are/were just speaking.

NOTE: When you use the particle **aṣ** (just), it must follow the auxiliary, and in this case, the auxiliary may come first in the sentence, contrary to our general rule.

THE IMPERFECTIVE AUXILIARY

The sentences with independent subject pronouns illustrate another fact about Papago. The form of the auxiliary is different when the pronoun is different. The forms of the imperfective auxiliary are listed below, with their corresponding subject pronouns. Note that the third person uses **'o** in both singular and plural.

	Singular			*Plural*		
	PRONOUN	AUX		PRONOUN	AUX	
1st per.	**('a:ñi)**	**'añ**	I am/was	**('a:cim)**	**'ac**	we are/were
2nd per.	**('a:pi)**	**'ap**	you are/were	**('a:pim)**	**'am**	you are/were
3rd per.	**(hegai)**	**'o**	he, she, it is/was	**(hegam)**	**'o**	they are/were

However, it is important to remember one fact about independent pronouns: an independent pronoun subject is only optionally present. In sentences where the independent pronoun is absent, the auxiliary still has all the possibilities in the table above. The examples in (1) through (6) above, then, can also be as follows:

7. **S-ba:bigĭ 'añ ñeok.** I am/was speaking slowly.
8. **S-hottam 'ap cipkan.** You were working quickly.
9. **Cicwi 'o.** He(she) is/was playing.
10. **Ganhu 'ac wo:po'ŏ.** We are/were running over there.
11. **'I:ya 'am cicwi.** You *(pl.)* are/were playing right here.
12. **'O 'aṣ ñeñok.** They are/were just speaking.

The following sentences are some more examples of the independent pronoun subject and the auxiliary:

13.	a. **’A:ñi ’añ s-hottam cipkan.** b. **S-hottam ’añ cipkan ’a:ñi.** c. **S-hottam ’añ cipkan.**	I am/was working quickly.
14.	a. **’A:pi ’ap s-ba:bigĭ him.** b. **S-ba:bigĭ ’ap him ’a:pi.** c. **S-ba:bigĭ ’ap him.**	You are/were walking slowly.
15.	a. **Hegai ’o tako ṣoak.** b. **Tako ’o ṣoak hegai.** c. **Tako ’o ṣoak.**	He/she was crying yesterday.
16.	a. **Hegam ’o s-hottam hihim.** b. **S-hottam ’o hihim hegam.** c. **S-hottam ’o hihim.**	They are/were walking quickly.
17.	a. **’A:pim ’am si s-kaidam ñeñok.** b. **Si ’am s-kaidam ñeñok ’a:pim.** c. **Si ’am s-kaidam ñeñok.**	You *(pl.)* are/were speaking very loudly.
18.	a. **Hegam ’o s-kaidam ṣoañ.** b. **S-kaidam ’o ṣoañ hegam.** c. **S-kaidam ’o ṣoañ.**	They are/were crying loudly.

INTERROGATIVE SENTENCES

Remember that the questions in Papago have the *question marker (QM)* **n-**, added to the auxiliary. The combinations of **n-** and the various forms of the auxiliary are listed below. Note that the initial glottal stop of the auxiliary is lost in the combined form.

QM	+	AUX	=	COMBINED FORM	QM	+	AUX	=	COMBINED FORM
n	+	**’añ**	=	**nañ**	**n**	+	**’ac**	=	**nac**
n	+	**’ap**	=	**nap**	**n**	+	**’am**	=	**nam**
n	+	**’o**	=	**no**	**n**	+	**’o**	=	**no**

The **n** + *aux* is always placed at the beginning of the question, as shown in the following example:

Nañ	**'a:ñi**	**ṣoak?**	
AUX	PRONOUN	VERB	
QM			Am/was I crying?
Nañ	**ṣoak**	**'a:ñi?**	
AUX	VERB	PRONOUN	
QM			

19. a. **No hegam hihim?** b. **No hihim hegam?** — Are/were they walking?

20. a. **Nap 'a:pi cipkan?** b. **Nap cipkan 'a:pi?** — Are/were you working?

21. a. **No ṣoak hegai 'ali?** b. **No hegai 'ali ṣoak?** — Is/was that baby crying?

22. a. **Nac 'a:cim wo:po'ŏ?** b. **Nac wo:po'ŏ 'a:cim?** — Are/were we running?

23. a. **Nam 'a:pim cicwi?** b. **Nam cicwi 'a:pim?** — Are/were you *(pl.)* playing?

24. a. **No hegam cecoj ñeñok?** b. **No ñeñok hegam cecoj?** — Are/were those boys speaking?

As shown earlier, the independent pronoun subject is only optionally present in statements; the same is true for questions.

25. a. **Nap 'a:pi ṣoak?** b. **Nap ṣoak?** — Are/were you crying?

26. a. **Nañ 'a:ñi cipkan?** b. **Nañ cipkan?** — Am/was I working?

27. a. **Nam 'a:pim ṣoañ?** b. **Nam ṣoañ?** — Are/were you *(pl.)* crying?

28. a. **Nac 'a:cim cicpkan?**
    b. **Nac cicpkan.**
    } Are/were we working?

29. a. **No 'ab meḍ hegai?**
    b. **No 'ab meḍ?**
    } Is/was he (she, it) running *(toward speaker)*?

30. a. **No 'am ki: hegam?**
    b. **No 'am ki:?**
    } Are/were they living there?

EXERCISES

A. In Lesson 2 we talked about the negative form of sentences, but all the sentences had noun subjects. Translate the following sentences with pronoun subjects into Papago. After translating these, give the *negative* version of the Papago sentence.

1. I am crying.
2. You are laughing.
3. They were working.
4. We are running.
5. She was sleeping.
6. He is walking.
7. You *(pl.)* were talking.
8. We were playing.

B. Translate the following questions into Papago:

1. Are you working?
2. Were they playing?
3. Is he speaking?
4. Are you *(pl.)* crying?
5. Was he sleeping?
6. Is it walking?
7. Were they running?
8. Is the dog crying?

C. Some of the sentences below contain errors and some are correct. For each of the following sentences indicate whether the sentence is correct or incorrect; and if it is incorrect, indicate what the error is.

1. Hegam gogs 'o ṣoañ.
2. 'Idam wipsilo ap hihim.
3. Nam hegai ceoj cipkan?
4. 'Idam mi:stol ap pi meḍ.
5. Hegai cecia o pi cicwi.
6. 'A:cim 'ac pi ko:ks.
7. Nap 'a:p ṣoak?
8. No 'idam 'o'odham hihim?

D. Rewrite the following sentences without using the independent pronouns:

1. 'A:ñi 'añ cipkan.
2. 'A:ñi 'añ s-ba:bigĭ ñeok.
3. Hegam 'o s-kaidam ṣoañ.
4. 'A:cim 'ac pi ṣa'i ko:kṣ.
5. No 'idam 'i:ya cicpkan?
6. 'A:pim 'am 'amai cicwi.
7. Hegai 'o ganhu meḍ.
8. 'A:pi 'ap 'i:ya ke:k.

LESSON 5

Conjunctions

VOCABULARY

NOUNS

Singular		*Plural*	
maistla	teacher	**mamaistla**	teachers
makai	doctor	**mamakai**	doctors
'e-maşcamdam	student	**'e-mamşcamdam**	students
'o'ohana	book	**'o'ohana**	books

VERBS

hehem	laughing	**hehem**	laughing
'oimeḍ	walking around	**'oyopo**	walking around
'o'ohan	writing, drawing	**'o'ohan**	writing, drawing

CONJOINING SIMPLE WORDS

In Papago the element **c** (and) is a conjunction which can be used to conjoin words, as in the following examples:

1. **Hegam 'e-mamşcam'dam c mamaistla 'o cicpkan.** Those students and teachers are/were working.
2. **Hegam gogogs c mimstol 'o wo:po'ŏ.** Those dogs and cats are/were running.
3. **'A'al 'o cicwi c hehem.** The children are/were playing and laughing.
4. **Gogs 'o meḍ c hi:nk.** The dog is/was running and barking.
5. **'A:ñi añ 'i:ya wo'o kc 'o'ohan.** I am/was lying here and writing.

6. **'A:pi c 'a:ñi 'ac 'i:ya 'oyopo.** You and I are/were walking around here.

NOTE: For some speakers of Papago, **c** is pronounced as **kc** when the preceding word ends in a vowel. In this case, example (6) above would be written: **'A:pi kc 'a:ñi 'ac 'i:ya 'oyopo.**

NOTE: If a determiner (e.g., **hegai, hegam, g**) refers to both conjoined nouns, as in samples (1) and (2) above, it is not repeated before the second noun.

Conjoined nouns are similar to plural nouns and take the plural auxiliaries, as follows:

Use **'ac** when the conjunction includes *first person:*

7. a. **'A:pi c 'a:ñi *'ac* ko:ks.** You and I are/were sleeping.

Use **'am** when the conjunction has *no first person* but has *second person:*

b. **'A:pi c Maliya *'am* si cicpkan.** You and Mary are/were really working.

And conjunctions of *third person* nouns always take **'o:**

c. **Mali:ya c Husi *'o* 'ab hihim.** Mary and Joe are/were walking this way.

CONJOINING SENTENCES

The following is an example of a conjoined sentence:

8. **'Uwĭ 'o cipkan ñ 'a:ñi ko:ṣ.** The woman is/was working and I am/was sleeping.

Example (8) is a combination of two sentences.

'Uwĭ 'o cipkan. + 'A:ñi 'añ ko:ṣ. The woman is/was working. + I am/was sleeping.

In conjoining two sentences, the second sentence must be changed: the auxiliary of the second sentence is placed at the beginning of the second sentence and its vowel is lost. For example:

'Uwĭ 'o cipkan. + 'A:ñi 'añ ko:ṣ.

'Uwĭ 'o cipkan + 'añ 'a:ñi ko:ṣ. *(Aux moves to beginning of second sentence)*

'Uwĭ 'o cipkan ñ 'a:ñi ko:ṣ. *(Aux drops its vowel)*

Notice that the auxiliary of the second sentence never appears in second position in the second sentence. That is, when the two sentences are conjoined, we never say:

***'Uwi 'o cipkan 'a:ñi 'añ ko:ṣ.**

In sentence (8) above, the second sentence has a first person singular subject. In (9), (10), and (11) below, the subject of the second sentence is second person singular, first person plural, and second person plural respectively. Otherwise these sentences follow the pattern for conjoined sentences we have just described. That is, the auxiliary of the second sentence is placed at the beginning of the second sentence and its vowel is lost.

9. **Ceoj 'o ñeok *p* 'a:pi aṣ hehem.** The boy is/was speaking and you are/were just laughing.
10. **'A'al 'o ṣoañ *c* 'a:cim ñeñok.** The children are/were crying and we are/were talking.
11. **'U'uwĭ 'o wo:po'ŏ *m* 'a:pim hihim.** The women are/were running and you *(pl.)* are/were walking.

Obviously, the form which is used depends on the appropriate form of the auxiliary for the second sentence. For example, sentence (9) is made up of the following two sentences:

Ceoj 'o ñeok. + 'A:pi 'ap ṣoak.

The auxiliary of the second sentence is moved to the beginning of the sentence and loses its vowel:

Ceoj 'o ñeok p 'a:pi ṣoak.

In example (10), **c** is derived from **'ac,** which is the auxiliary appropriate for the second sentence. In example (11), **m** is derived from **'am,** which is the auxiliary appropriate for the second sentence.

In conjoined sentences in which the second sentence has a third person subject [e.g., **hegai** (he/she/it) or **hegam** (they)], the situation is a little bit different. Sentences with a third person subject have the auxiliary **'o.**

12. **Hegai ceoj 'o 'oimeḍ.** That boy is/was walking around.

13. **Hegam mimstol 'o cicwi.** Those cats are/were playing.

However, conjoined sentences in which the subject of the second sentence is third person (singular or plural) have the form illustrated in (14) and (15).

14. **Kawyu 'o meḍ k hegai ceoj him.** The horse is/was running and that boy is/was walking.
15. **Gogogs 'o hihink k hegam mimstol cicwi.** The dogs are/were barking and those cats are/were playing.

That is, when the aux **'o** moves to the beginning of the second conjoined sentence, it changes to **k.**

The table below summarizes the special forms of the auxiliary illustrated in conjoined sentences.

	Singular	*Plural*
1st person	**ñ**	**c**
2nd person	**p**	**m**
3rd person	**k**	**k**

Be sure to insert the **g** determiner when conjoining sentences such as:

'Uwĭ 'o cipkan. + Makai 'o ñeok. The woman is/was working + The doctor is/was speaking.
'Uwĭ 'o cipkan k *g* makai ñeok.

Recall that the **g** determiner drops out only at the very beginning of a sentence, but remains if other words precede it.

Some speakers of Papago add **ku-** to the first and second persons of the special forms of the auxiliary at the beginning of the second sentence in a conjoined sentence, as shown below:

'Uwĭ 'o cipkan *kuñ* 'a:ñi 'o'ohan. The woman is/was working and I am/was writing.

Mamakai 'o ñeñok *kup* 'a:pi ṣoak. The doctors are/were speaking and you are/were crying.

'A'al 'o ṣoañ *kuc* 'a:cim ñeñok. The children are/were crying and we are/were speaking.

Some speakers of Papago use **c** to conjoin all sentences as well as to conjoin simple words. For example, instead of (1) below, these speakers use (2):

1. **'Uwĭ 'o cipkan ñ 'a:ñi ko:ṣ.**
2. **'Uwĭ 'o cipkan *c* 'a:ñi ko:ṣ.**

} The woman is/was working and I am/was sleeping.

But notice that the auxiliary of the second sentence is dropped out; the following is never said:

***'Uwĭ 'o cipkan *c* 'a:ñi 'añ ko:ṣ.**

EXERCISES

A. Translate into Papago, using the conjunction **c**:

1. Mary and Frank are walking around here.
2. The women were talking and laughing.
3. The cows and the calves are sleeping.
4. The doctor is writing.
5. Albert and Peter and you were writing.

B. On a separate sheet of paper conjoin the following sentences:

Example

'A:ñi 'añ cipkan. + 'A:pi 'ap aṣ cicwi.
'A:ñi 'añ cipkan *p* 'a:pi aṣ cicwi.

1. Kawyu 'o meḍ. + Wisilo 'o ko:ṣ.
2. 'A:cim 'ac si cicpkan. + 'A:pim 'am aṣ cicwi.
3. Gogs 'o hi:nk. + Mi:stol 'o cicwi.
4. 'A:pi 'ap ñeok. + 'A:ñi 'añ pi ñeok.
5. Wo:po'ŏ 'o g hahaiwañ. + Gogogs 'o hihink.
6. Si 'o meḍ g 'uwĭ. + Ceoj 'o aṣ him.
7. Hegam 'o aṣ ko:kṣ. + 'A:cim 'ac cicpkan.
8. 'A:cim 'ac aṣ cicwi. + 'A:pim 'am si cicpkan.

C. Translate into Papago:

1. The teachers are writing and the students are reading.
2. The babies were laughing and the dogs were barking.

3. You are working and I am just talking.
4. We are working and you are just talking.
5. I was working and you and Mary were just talking.
6. Those girls are working and you and I are just talking.
7. They are working here and the doctors are working over there.
8. We are working and Mary and the boys are just talking.

D. *For native speakers only.* Make up at least five sentences with natural word orders and natural conjunction forms. In the sentences that you make up, do you find any new elements that we have not discussed yet? How would you try to explain these new elements to someone who is not a native speaker of Papago?

Direct and Indirect Objects in Transitive Sentences

VOCABULARY

NOUNS

Singular		*Plural*	
ban	coyote	**ba:ban**	coyotes
cu:wĭ	jackrabbit	**cu:wĭ**	jackrabbits
daikuḍ	chair	**dadaikuḍ**	chairs
ha'icu	something, thing	**ha'icu**	things
ki:	house, home	**ki:k, ki:kĭ**	houses
ma:gina	car, machine	**mamgina**	cars, machines
mi:sa	table	**mimsa**	tables
nalaṣ	orange	**nalaṣ**	oranges
to:bĭ	rabbit, cottontail	**totobĭ**	rabbits, cottontails
wakial	cowboy	**wapkial**	cowboys

VERBS

a:gid	saying, telling	**a:gid**	saying, telling
ceggia	fighting	**ceggia**	fighting
cendad	kissing	**cendad**	kissing
ceposid	branding	**cecposid**	branding
gatwid	shooting	**gagtwid**	shooting
huhu'id	chasing	**huhu'id**	chasing
ka:	hearing	**ka:**	hearing
kegcid	cleaning	**kegcid**	cleaning
ma:k	giving	**mamk**	giving
ñeid	seeing	**ñeid**	seeing
ñu:kud	taking care of	**ñu:kud**	taking care of
ṣa:mud	herding, shooing away	**ṣa:mud**	herding, shooing away
wakon	washing	**wapkon**	washing

OTHER EXPRESSIONS

we:hejeḍ for

DIRECT OBJECTS IN SIMPLE TRANSITIVE SENTENCES

The following are examples of simple transitive sentences:

1. **Ban 'o huhu'id g cu:wĭ.** The coyote is/was chasing the jackrabbit.
2. **Cehia 'o ñu:kud g 'ali.** The girl is/was taking care of the child.

A simple transitive sentence has—in addition to a subject, an aux, and a verb—a direct object, which receives the action of the verb.

Ban	**'o**	**huhu'id**	**g cu:wĭ.**
SUBJECT	AUX	VERB	OBJECT

Cehia	**'o**	**ñu:kud**	**g 'ali.**
SUBJECT	AUX	VERB	OBJECT

In sentences (1) and (2) the order of these elements is: subject, aux, verb, direct object. But, except for the fact that the aux must be second, the order of elements in a simple transitive sentence does not have to be like that shown in (1) and (2); in fact, any possible order of subject, object and verb is a good Papago sentence. Sentences (3a) through (3e) give all the other possible word orders for sentence (1).

3. a. **Huhu'id 'o g ban g cu:wĭ.**
VERB AUX SUBJECT OBJECT
b. **Ban 'o g cu:wĭ huhu'id.**
SUBJECT AUX OBJECT VERB
c. **Cu:wĭ 'o huhu'id g ban.**
OBJECT AUX VERB SUBJECT
d. **Huhu'id 'o g cu:wĭ g ban.**
VERB AUX OBJECT SUBJECT
e. **Cu:wĭ 'o g ban huhu'id.**
OBJECT AUX SUBJECT VERB

} The coyote is/was chasing the jackrabbit.

The following examples give all the other possible word orders for sentence (2):

4. a. **Ñu:kud 'o g 'ali g cehia.**
VERB AUX OBJECT SUBJECT

b.	**Cehia**	**'o**	**g 'ali**	**ñu:kud.**	The girl is/was taking care of the child.
	SUBJECT	AUX	OBJECT	VERB	
c.	**'Ali**	**'o**	**ñu:kud**	**g cehia.**	
	OBJECT	AUX	VERB	SUBJECT	
d.	**Ñu:kud**	**'o**	**g cehia**	**g 'ali.**	
	VERB	AUX	SUBJECT	OBJECT	
e.	**'Ali**	**'o**	**g cehia**	**ñu:kud.**	
	OBJECT	AUX	SUBJECT	VERB	

NOTE: Occasionally this flexibility of word order can make the meaning of a sentence ambiguous. For example, "**Ceoj 'o g gogs huhu'id**" can mean either "The boy is chasing the dog" or "The dog is chasing the boy." In such cases the native speaker uses different devices in order to get the correct or appropriate meaning for the sentence. These devices include the context of the sentence, increased stress on the subject of the sentence, and the intonation of the entire sentence, which will in some cases give clues as to which is the subject and which is the object.

The following are more examples of simple transitive sentences:

5. a. **Wisilo 'o ṣa:mud hegai wakial.**
   b. **Hegai wakial 'o g wisilo ṣa:mud.**
   c. **Ṣa:mud 'o g wisilo hegai wakial.**

   That cowboy is/was herding the calf.

6. a. **Ceposid 'añ 'a:ñi g haiwañ.**
   b. **Ceposid 'añ g haiwañ 'a:ñi.**
   c. **'A:ñi 'añ g haiwañ ceposid.**

   I am/was branding a cow.

7. a. **Kegcid 'ac g ki: 'a:cim.**
   b. **'A:cim 'ac g ki: kegcid.**
   c. **Ki: 'ac kegcid 'a:cim.**

   We are/were cleaning the house.

PLURAL DIRECT OBJECTS

The direct objects in examples (1) through (7) are singular. In sentences (8) through (12) the objects of the verbs are plural. When an object is plural, we must prefix **ha-** to the verb in the sentence; this prefix simply indicates that the object of the verb is plural.

NOTE: In transitive sentences the aux agrees in number with the subject, but the verb agrees in number with the direct object.

Examples

A:cim	**ac**	**g**	**wisilo**	**ceposid.**
SUBJECT	AUX	DET	DIRECT OBJECT	VERB
(pl.)	*(pl.)*		*(sg.)*	*(sg.)*
We	are/were	the	calf	branding.

A:ñi	**añ**	**g**	**wipsilo**	**ha-cecposid.**
SUBJECT	AUX	DET	DIRECT OBJECT	VERB
(sg.)	*(sg.)*		*(pl.)*	*(pl.)*
I	am/was	the	calves	branding.

8. a. **Ban 'o g totobĭ ha-huhu'id.**
   b. **Ha-huhu'id 'o g ban g totobĭ.**
   c. **Ha-huhu'id 'o g totobĭ g ban.**

   The coyote is/was chasing the cottontails.

9. a. **Cehia 'o ha-wapkon g mamgina.**
   b. **Ha-wapkon 'o g mamgina g cehia.**
   c. **Mamgina 'o ha-wapkon g cehia.**

   The girl is/was washing the cars.

10. a. **Wakial 'o g wipsilo ha-ṣa:mud.**
    b. **Wipsilo 'o ha-ṣa:mud g wakial.**
    c. **Ha-ṣa:mud 'o g wipsilo g wakial.**

    The cowboy is/was herding the calves.

11. a. **Ha-cecposid 'añ a:ñi g hahaiwañ.**
    b. **'A:ñi 'añ g hahaiwañ ha-cecposid.**
    c. **Hahaiwañ 'añ ha-cecposid 'a:ñi.**

    I am/was branding the cows.

12. a. **'A:cim 'ac ha-ñeid g ki:k.**
    b. **Ha-ñeid 'ac g ki:k 'a:cim.**
    c. **Ki:k 'ac ha-ñeid 'a:cim.**

    We see/saw the houses. (*Literal:* We are/were seeing the houses.)

The following are more examples of transitive sentences with singular and plural objects:

13. a. **Huan 'o ceggia g Husi.**
    b. **Ceggia 'o g Huan g Husi.**
    c. **Huan 'o g Husi ceggia.**

    John is/was fighting Joe.

14. a. **Wakial 'o ha-ñu:kud g hahaiwañ.**
    b. **Ha-ñu:kud 'o g hahaiwañ g wakial.**
    c. **Wakial 'o g hahaiwañ ha-ñu:kud.**

    The cowboy is/was taking care of the cows.

15. a. **Huan 'o cendad g Mali:ya.**
    b. **Huan 'o g Mali:ya cendad.**
    c. **Mali:ya 'o cendad g Huan.**
    } John is/was kissing Mary.

16. a. **'Uwĭ 'o ha-kegcid g mimsa.**
    b. **Ha-kegcid 'o g mimsa g 'uwĭ.**
    c. **'Uwĭ 'o g mimsa ha-kegcid.**
    } The woman is/was cleaning the tables.

17. a. **Mimstol 'o ha-huhu'id g gogs.**
    b. **Gogs 'o g mimstol ha-huhu'id.**
    c. **Ha-huhu'id 'o g mimstol g gogs.**
    } The dog is/was chasing the cats.

Note that only a plural *object* of the verb causes **ha-** to be added to the verb. A plural *subject* in a sentence does not cause **ha-** to be added to the verb. Sentences (18) and (19), for example, have plural subjects and singular objects; the verbs do not have the **ha-** prefix.

18. ***Cecia* 'o ñu:kud *g 'ali.*** The *girls* are taking care of the *baby.*

19. ***Cecoj* 'o ceposid *g haiwañ.*** The *boys* are branding the *cow.*

PRONOUN DIRECT OBJECTS

All the objects in the examples above have been nouns. It is also possible to have pronoun direct objects. For example,

20. a. **Gogs 'o hegai huhu'id.**
    b. **Gogs 'o huhu'id hegai.**
    c. **Huhu'id 'o hegai g gogs.**
    } The dog is/was chasing it (that, her, him.)

21. a. **Gogs 'o ha-huhu'id hegam.**
    b. **Gogs 'o hegam ha-huhu'id.**
    c. **Ha-huhu'id 'o g gogs hegam.**
    } The dog is/was chasing them (those).

The pronoun direct objects, which have the same *form* as subject pronouns, are given below:

	Singular		*Plural*	
1st person	**'a:ñi**	me	**'a:cim**	us
2nd person	**'a:pi**	you	**'a:pim**	you
3rd person	**hegai**	him, her, it, that	**hegam**	them, those

As examples (20) and (21) show, the third person singular and the third person plural pronoun objects act just like singular and plural noun objects. The pronoun **hegam,** as an object, requires that the prefix **ha-** be on the verb; the pronoun **hegai,** as an object, does not require a prefix on the verb.

The other pronoun direct objects all require a prefix on the verb; these prefixes are given in the table below:

	Singular	*Plural*
1st person	**ñ-**	**t-**
2nd person	**m-**	**'em-**
3rd person	– (no prefix)	**ha-**

In using first and second person pronouns as objects of a sentence, the following rule is used:

When **'a:ñi** is the object, use **ñ-** + verb;

When **'a:pi** is the object, use **m-** + verb;

When **'a:cim** is the object, use **t-** + verb;

When **'a:pim** is the object, use **'em-** + verb.

The following are examples of sentences with first and second person direct objects.

22. a. **Ceoj 'o 'a:ñi ñ-ceggia.**
    b. **'A:ñi 'o ñ-ceggia g ceoj.**
    c. **Ñ-ceggia 'o 'a:ñi g ceoj.**
    } The boy is/was fighting me.

23. a. **Klisti:na 'o 'a:pi m-cendad.**
    b. **M-cendad 'o 'a:pi g Klisti:na.**
    c. **'A:pi 'o m-cendad g Klisti:na.**
    } Christina is/was kissing you.

24. a. **Hegai 'ali 'o 'a:cim t-kuḍut.**
    b. **T-kuḍut 'o hegai 'ali a:cim.**
    c. **'A:cim 'o t-kuḍut hegai 'ali.**

    } That child is/was bothering us.

25. a. **Hegai 'uwĭ 'o 'a:pim 'em-ñu:kud.**
    b. **'A:pim 'o 'em-ñu:kud hegai 'uwĭ.**
    c. **'Em-ñu:kud 'o 'a:pim hegai 'uwĭ.**

    } That woman is/was taking care of you *(pl.)*.

Just like independent pronoun *subjects,* independent pronoun *objects* are only optionally present in Papago transitive sentences. So, examples (26) through (31) below are like (20) through (25) except that (26) through (31) lack independent pronoun objects.

26. **Gogs 'o huhu'id.** The dog is/was chasing it (that, her, him).
27. **Gogs 'o ha-huhu'id.** The dog is/was chasing them (those).
28. **Ceoj 'o ñ-ceggia.** The boy is/was fighting me.
29. **Klisti:na 'o m-cendad.** Christina is/was kissing you.
30. **Hegai 'ali 'o t-kuḍut.** That child is/was bothering us.
31. **Hegai 'uwĭ 'o 'em-ñu:kud.** That woman is/was taking care of you *(pl.)*.

INDIRECT OBJECT

It is also possible for transitive Papago sentences to have an indirect object (I.O.) This indirect object, which is always some noun or pronoun, states *to whom* or *for whom* something is done. The following gives a breakdown of the structure of a transitive sentence containing an indirect object:

Husi	**'o**	**kegcid**	**g nalaṣ**	**g 'ali**	**wehejeḍ.**
SUBJECT	AUX	VERB	D.O.	I.O.	for

Joe is/was cleaning the orange for the child.

Like the other transitive sentences that we saw, it is also possible for these sentences with indirect objects to have more than one word order. The following sentences show the alternate word orders for the example above:

'Ali we:hejeḍ 'o kegcid g nalaṣ g Husi.

Nalaṣ 'o kegcid g Husi g 'ali we:hejeḍ.

Kegcid 'o g nalaṣ g 'ali we:hejeḍ g Husi.

Joe is/was cleaning the orange for the child.

Other examples of transitive sentences with both direct and indirect objects are shown below:

32. a. **Husi 'o wakon g ma:gina g Huan we:hejeḍ.**
    b. **Ma:gina 'o wakon g Husi g Huan we:hejeḍ.**
    c. **Huan we:hejeḍ 'o wakon g ma:gina g Husi.**
    d. **Husi ' g ma:gina wakon g Huan we:hejeḍ.**

    Joe is/was washing the car for John.

33. a. **'A:ñi 'añ ma:k g o'ohana g Husi.**
    b. **Husi 'añ ma:k g 'o'ohana.**
    c. **'O'ohana añ ma:k g Husi.**

    I am/was giving the book to Joe. (Or, I am/was giving Joe the book.)

34. a. **Huan 'o ha'icu 'a:gid g Mali:ya.**
    b. **Huan 'o g Mali:ya ha'icu a:gid.**
    c. **Ha'icu 'o 'a:gid g Mali:ya g Huan.**

    John is/was telling something to Mary. (Or, John is/was telling Mary something.)

NOTE: The word "for" (**wehejeḍ**) is expressed in these sentences, but the word "to" is simply implied or understood in Papago.

If the indirect object is a pronoun, it is attached as a prefix either to **wehejeḍ,** if it is present, or to the verb. The pronouns, which are the same as the special prefix forms for the direct object pronouns, are listed below:

	Singular		*Plural*	
1st person	**n-**	(to, for) me	**t-**	(to, for) us
2nd person	**m-**	(to, for) you	**'em-**	(to, for) you
3rd person	—	(no prefix)	**ha-**	(to, for) them

The following are examples of sentences with indirect object pronouns:

35. a. **Mali:ya 'o ha-ñu:kud 'g 'a'al ñ-we:hejeḍ.**
    b. **Ñ-we:hejeḍ 'o ha-ñu:kud g 'a'al g Mali:ya.**
    c. **Ha-ñu:kud 'o g 'a'al g Mali:ya ñ-we:hejeḍ.**
    d. **Mali:ya 'o g 'a'al ha-ñu:kud ñ-we:hejeḍ.**

    Mary is/was taking care of the children for me.

36. a. **Husi 'o t-ma:k g daikuḍ.**
    b. **Husi 'o g daikuḍ t-ma:k.**
    c. **T-ma:k 'o daikuḍ g Husi.**

    Joe is giving us a chair. (Or, Joe is giving a chair to us.)

NOTE: The plural direct object marker **ha-** is dropped if the indirect object pronoun has to attach to the verb (e.g., in sentences in which "to" is implied). It is retained if the sentence contains "for," since the indirect object pronoun can attach to **wehejed.**

37. a. **Mali:ya 'o ha-wapkon g mamgina 'em-we:hejeḍ.**
    b. **Mali:ya 'o g mamgina ha-wapkon 'em-we:hejeḍ.**
    c. **'Em-we:hejeḍ 'o ha-wapkon g mamgina g Mali:ya.**

    Mary is/was washing cars for you *(pl.)*.

38. a. **A:ñi 'añ ha-mamk g mimsa.**
    b. **Ha-mamk 'añ ('a:ñi) g mimsa.**
    c. **Mimsa 'añ (a:ñi) ha-mamk.**
    d. **A:ñi 'añ g mimsa ha-mamk.**

    I am/was giving them the tables. (Or, I am/was giving the tables to them.)

EXERCISES

A. Translate the following examples into English:

1. a. No g 'ali m-kuḍut?
   b. Heu'u, ñ-kuḍut 'o g 'ali.
   c. Pi'a, pi 'o ñ-kuḍut g 'ali.
2. a. No 'em-kuḍut hegai gogs?
   b. Pi'a, pi 'o t-kuḍut hegai gogs.
   c. Heu'u, t-kuḍut 'o hegai gogs.

3. a. Gogogs 'o 'a:cim t-huhu'id.
   b. Gogogs 'o t-huhu'id.
4. a. 'Ali 'o 'a:pi m-ñeid.
   b. 'Ali 'o m-ñeid.
5. a. 'A:ñi 'añ ñ-ñeid.
   b. Ñ-ñeid 'añ.

B. Translate into Papago:

1. Are you herding the horses for us?
2. The woman was taking care of the boys and the girls.
3. The child is taking care of the dog and the girl is herding the cows.
4. Joe is giving the oranges to you *(sg.)*.
5. The dog was barking and chasing the cat.
6. The boy is laughing and the child is crying.
7. I am working and you *(sg.)* are crying.
8. The cowboy is herding the calves.
9. The coyote was chasing the jackrabbit.
10. Mary is giving me the table and a chair.

C. Translate into English:

1. Cecia 'o ha-huhu'id g totobĭ.
2. 'Ali 'o ha-ṣa:mud g wipsilo.
3. No g wakial ha-cecposid g kakawyu?
4. No g gogs ha-huhu'id g mimstol?
5. No g wapkial ha-cecposid g wipsilo?
6. Ceoj 'o ha-ñu:kud g 'a'al.
7. 'A:cim 'ac ko:kṣ kum 'a:pim cicpkan.
8. Gogogs 'o wo:po'ŏ k g kakawyu hihim.

D. Rewrite the following sentences on a sheet of paper and fill in the blanks with one or more appropriate Papago word or words.

1. __________ 'o huhu'id g cu:wĭ.
2. Cehia 'o __________ g ali.
3. Hegai wakial 'o ṣa:mud g __________ .
4. __________ 'añ ha-cecposid g hahaiwañ.

5. Wapkial 'o __________ g haiwañ.
6. Gogs 'o ñeid g __________ .
7. 'A:cim __________ ñeñok __________ cicpkan.
8. Uwĭ 'o __________ c __________ .

E. Translate into Papago using the correct conjunction form:
1. The boy and I are herding the cows.
2. The woman is working and the man is taking care of the baby for Mary.
3. The coyote was chasing the boy and the boy was crying.
4. The cow is running and the cowboy is chasing it.
5. The girl is walking and singing.
6. The baby sees (is seeing) the chair and the table.
7. You *(pl.)* and they hear (are hearing) the car.

LESSON 7

Reflexives and Reciprocals

VOCABULARY

VERBS

Singular		*Plural*	
dagkon	wiping, drying	**dadagkon**	wiping, drying
'eñigadad	dressing, getting dressed	**'e'eñigadad**	dressing, getting dressed
gaswua	combing hair	**gagswua**	combing hair
gegosid	eating, feeding	**gegosid**	eating, feeding
hikck	cutting	**hihikck,** or **hikc**	cutting
hu:kajid	warming	**hu:kajid**	warming
hukṣan	scratching	**huhukṣan**	scratching
ka:	hearing, listening to	**ka:**	hearing, listening to
keihin	kicking	**keihin**	kicking
wacwi	bathing, swimming	**wapcwi**	bathing, swimming

OTHER EXPRESSIONS

'a'i each other

REFLEXIVE PREFIXES

The following examples illustrate a reflexive sentence:

1. a. **'A:pi 'ap 'e-wakon.**
   b. **'E-wakon 'ap 'a:pi.**
   c. **'E-wakon 'ap.**
   } You are/were washing yourself.

A reflexive sentence contains a verb with a reflexive prefix. For example, **wakon** (wash) in (1) has the prefix **'e.** The following is a table of all the reflexive prefixes:

	Singular		*Plural*	
1st person	**ñ-**	myself	**t-**	ourselves
2nd person	**'e-**	yourself	**'e-**	yourselves
3rd person	**'e-**	himself, herself, itself	**'e-**	themselves

The reflexive prefix must agree with the subject of the sentence. So, when the subject of the sentence is second person singular, as in (1), the reflexive prefix is **'e**. Example (2) shows a reflexive sentence with a first person singular subject, for which the reflexive prefix is **ñ**.

2. a. **'A:ñi 'añ ñ-gegosid.**
   b. **Ñ-gegosid 'añ 'a:ñi.**
   c. **Ñ-gegosid 'añ.**
   } I am/was eating (*Literal:* I am/was feeding myself.)

Examples (3) through (11) show more reflexive sentences.

3. a. **Hegam 'o 'e-hu:kajid.**
   b. **'E-hu:kajid 'o hegam.**
   c. **'E-hu:kajid 'o.**
   } They are/were warming themselves.
4. a. **Gogs 'o 'e-hukṣan.**
   b. **'E-hukṣan 'o g gogs.**
   } The dog is/was scratching itself.
5. a. **Ceoj 'o 'e-ka:.**
   b. **'E-ka: 'o g ceoj.**
   } The boy is/was hearing himself.
6. a. **A:cim 'ac t-e'eñigadad.**
   b. **T-e'eñigadad 'ac a:cim.**
   c. **T-e'eñigadad 'ac.**
   } We are/were getting dressed.
7. a. **'Ali 'o 'e-hikck.**
   b. **'E-hikck 'o g 'ali.**
   } The child is/was cutting himself.
8. a. **'A'al 'o 'e-dadagkon.**
   b. **'E-dadagkon 'o g 'a'al.**
   } The children are/were drying themselves.
9. a. **'U'uwĭ 'o 'e-e'eñigadad.**
   b. **'E-e'eñigadad 'o g 'u'uwĭ.**
   } The women are/were getting dressed.
10. a. **Cehia 'o 'e-gaswua.**
    b. **'E-gaswua 'o g cehia.**
    } The girl is/was combing her hair (*literal* herself).
11. a. **Hegam cecoj 'o 'e-wapcwi.**
    b. **'E-wapcwi 'o hegam cecoj.**
    } Those boys are/were bathing.

RECIPROCAL SENTENCES

The following illustrates a reciprocal sentence:

12. a. **'A'al 'o 'a'i 'e-wapkon.**
    b. **'A'i 'o 'e-wapkon g 'a'al.**
    } The children are/were washing each other.

A reciprocal sentence, like a reflexive sentence, contains a reflexive prefix on the verb (e.g., **'e-wapkon**); however, the reciprocal sentence also contains the word **'a'i** (each other).

13. a. **'A'al 'o 'a'i 'e-wapkon.**
    b. **'A'i 'o 'e-wapkon g 'a'al.**
    } The children are/were washing each other.
14. a. **Cecia 'o 'a'i 'e-huhukṣan.**
    b. **'A'i 'o 'e-huhukṣan g cecia.**
    } The girls are/were scratching each other.
15. a. **Gogogs 'o 'a'i 'e-huhu'id.**
    b. **'A'i 'o 'e-huhu'id g gogogs.**
    } The dogs are/were chasing each other.
16. a. **Kakawyu 'o 'a'i 'e-keihin.**
    b. **'A'i 'o 'e-keihin g kakawyu.**
    } The horses are/were kicking each other.
17. a. **Cecoj 'o 'a'i 'e-ka:.**
    b. **'A'i 'o 'e-ka: g cecoj.**
    } The boys are/were listening to each other.
18. a. **'A'al 'o 'a'i 'e-dadagkon.**
    b. **'A'i 'o 'e-dadagkon g 'a'al.**
    } The children are/were drying each other.
19. a. **Cecia 'o 'a'i 'e-'e'eñigadad.**
    b. **'A'i 'o 'e'eñigadad g cecia.**
    } The girls are/were dressing each other.
20. a. **'U'uwĭ 'o 'a'i 'e-gagswua.**
    b. **'A'i 'o 'e-gagswua g 'u'uwĭ.**
    } The women are/were combing each other's hair.

EXERCISES

A. Translate into English:

1. 'Idam 'u'uwĭ 'o 'e-wapcwi.
2. Hegam cecoj c cecia 'o a'i 'e-ñeid.
3. 'A:ñi 'añ ñ-keihin.
4. No g 'o'odham 'e-'eñigadad?

5. Pi 'o 'e-gaswua 'i:da cehia.
6. Hegai 'ali 'o pi 'e-ka.
7. Heu'u, 'e-gegosid 'o g kawyu.
8. 'A:ñi 'añ ñ-gegosid.

B. Rewrite the following sentences on a separate sheet of paper and fill in the appropriate verb form.

1. 'I:da haiwañ 'o __________ (seeing itself)
2. Ceoj 'o __________ (eating, feeding himself)
3. Cecia c 'u'uwĭ 'o __________ (combing their hair)
4. 'A:ñi 'añ __________ (scratching myself)
5. 'A:pi c 'a:ñi 'ac __________ (seeing each other)
6. 'A:cim 'ac __________ (wiping ourselves dry)
7. 'A:pim 'am __________ (cutting yourselves)

LESSON 8

Postpositional Phrases and Locatives

VOCABULARY

NOUNS

Singular		*Plural*	
Cuk Ṣon	Tucson	—	
daikuḍ	chair	**dadaikuḍ**	chairs
do'ag	mountain	**do'ag**	mountains
ju:kĭ	rain	—	
kui	mesquite, tree	**kukui**	mesquites, trees
maṣcamakuḍ	school	**mamaṣcamakuḍ**	schools
tianda	store	**titianda**	stores
to:nk	hill	**totonk**	hills
wo'ikuḍ	bed	**wo:po'ikuḍ**	beds

VERBS

dahă	sitting	**dadhă**, or **daḍhă**	sitting
ke:k	standing	**gegok**	standing

POSTPOSITIONS

ba'ic in front of (a person)
ba:ṣo in front of (a thing)
da:m on top
hugidan next to
we:big behind
weco under
wui to, toward

LOCATIVES

'amai, 'am over there (*in front of speaker*)
'anai, 'an over there (*next to speaker*)
gaḍhu, gḍhu over there (*out of sight of speaker*)
ganhu, gnhu over there (*in sight of speaker*)
'eḍa, 'eḍ inside, in
'i:ma, 'im back here, there (*in back of speaker*)
'i:ya, 'i right here

SPECIFIERS AND POSTPOSITIONS

The following are examples of postpositional phrases:

'am ki: ba:ṣo in front of the house

'am mi:sa ba:ṣo in front of the table

'am ma:gina ba:ṣo in front of the car

Each of these examples contains some noun (e.g., **ki:**). The noun is preceded by **'am,** which is a *specifier* of the postpositional phrase, and is followed by **ba:ṣo** which is called a *postposition.*

NOTE: *Postpositions* in Papago correspond to *prepositions* in English. Their function is the same, but they follow, rather than precede, their objects—hence they are *post*positions. Postpositional phrases generally begin with a specifier and end with a postposition. The following is an analysis of a sentence which contains a postpositional phrase:

'Uwĭ	**'o**	**'am**	**ki:**	ba:ṣo	**ke:k.**
NOUN	AUX	SPECIFIER	NOUN	POSTPOSITION	VERB

The woman is/was standing in front of the house.

NOTE: Normally when a noun appears in a sentence it is preceded by the "**g**" determiner. However, when the noun is *within* a postpositional phrase, it is directly preceded by a specifier and the "**g**" is dropped. (If the object of the postposition is located *outside* the postpositional phrase, the "**g**" determiner is used as usual. See Chapter 20 on word order.)

Here are more postpositional phrases:

1. ***'Am. . .we:big***	behind
a. **'Am ki: we:big**	behind the house
b. **'Am do'ag we:big**	behind the mountain
c. **'Am kui we:big**	behind the tree
2. ***An. . .da:m***	on top of, over, above
a. **'An mi:sa da:m**	on top of the table
b. **'An do'ag da:m**	on top of the mountain
c. **'An ṣu:dagĭ da:m**	on top of the water
3. ***'Am. . .weco***	under, beneath
a. **'Am daikuḍ weco**	under the chair
b. **'Am wo'ikuḍ weco**	under the bed
c. **'Am mi:sa weco**	under the table
4. ***'Am. . .ba'ic***	in front of (a person)
a. **'Am Husi ba'ic**	in front of Joe
b. **'Am Mali:ya ba'ic**	in front of Mary
c. **'Am Huan ba'ic**	in front of John
5. ***Ab. . .wui***	to, toward
a. **'Ab Cuk Ṣon wui**	to, toward Tucson
b. **'Ab Mali:ya wui**	to, toward Mary
c. **'Ab Huan wui**	to, toward John
6. ***An. . .hugidan***	next to
a. **'An ki: hugidan**	next to the house
b. **'An Husi hugidan**	next to Joe
c. **'An kawyu hugidan**	next to the horse

SPECIFIERS AS INDICATORS OF DIRECTION

Notice that the postpositional phrases above are given with one of three different specifiers — **'ab, 'am,** or **'an.** Each of these three specifiers indicates a different position, relative to the speaker, of the object of the postposition. For example:

Example	*Movement*
A. **Huan 'o *'am* Cuk Ṣon wui him.** John is/was walking to Tucson.	(*away from* the speaker)
B. **Huan 'o *'ab* Cuk Ṣon wui him.** John is/was walking to Tucson.	(*toward* the speaker)
C. **Huan 'o *'an* Cuk Ṣon wui him.** John is/was walking to Tucson.	(*parallel to* the speaker)

In example (A) **'am** indicates movement away from the speaker—i.e., John is walking to Tucson in a direction away from the speaker. In (B) **'ab** indicates movement toward the speaker. In (C) **'an** indicates movement from one point to another in a direction parallel to the speaker—i.e. John is walking to Tucson (from another point) in a direction parallel to where the speaker is. **'Am** always indicates an orientation away from the speaker; **'ab** always indicates an orientation toward the speaker; and **'an** always indicates an orientation next to the speaker. However, as shown in the examples below (D–F), these words may indicate *location,* rather than actual *movement.*

Example	*Location*
D. **Husi 'o *'am* ki: ba:ṣo ke:k.** Joe is/was standing in front of the house.	(*away from* the speaker)
E. **Husi 'o *'ab* ki: ba:ṣo ke:k.** Joe is/was standing in front of the house.	(*toward* the speaker, or *facing* the speaker)
F. **Husi 'o *'an* ki: ba:ṣo ke:k.** Joe is/was standing in front of the house.	(*next to* the speaker, side by side)

Sentences (G), (H), and (I) are three more examples of the locational use of **'am, 'ab,** and **'an.**

Example	*Location*
G. **Mali:ya 'o *'am* Klisti:na ba'ic ke:k.** Mary is/was standing in front of Christina.	(*away from* the speaker, *facing away from* the speaker)
H. **Mali:ya 'o *'ab* Klisti:na ba'ic ke:k.** Mary is/was standing in front of Christina.	(*toward* the speaker, *facing toward* the speaker)
I. **Mali:ya 'o *'an* Klisti:na we:big ke:k.** Mary is/was standing behind Christina.	(*next to, in back of* the speaker)

To summarize, **'am** is used when the movement is away from the speaker or when the point of location is away from the speaker; **'ab** is used when the movement is toward the speaker or when the point of location is facing the speaker; and **'an** is used when the movement is parallel to the speaker or when the point of location is on a line parallel to the position of the speaker relative to a third object.

POSTPOSITIONAL OBJECTS

Every postpositional phrase up to now has had a noun object; however, it is possible for a postpositional phrase to have a pronoun object. Below are the forms of pronouns which are the objects of postpositions. If used, these pronouns attach as prefixes to the postposition word.

	Singular		*Plural*	
1st person	**ñ-**	me	**t-**	us
2nd person	**m-**	you	**'em-**	you
3rd person	**ha-**	him, her, it, that	**ha-**	them, those

The following are examples:

7. **Mali:ya 'o 'am ñ-ba'ic dahă.** Mary is/was sitting in front of me.
8. **Ju:kĭ 'o 'ab t-wui him.** The rain is coming (*literally* walking) toward us.
9. **Huan 'o 'am 'em-wui him.** John is/was walking toward you (*pl.*).
10. **Klisti:na 'o 'an ha-hugidan dahă.** Christina is/was sitting next to them.

WORD ORDER IN POSTPOSITIONAL PHRASES

Consider the pair of sentences in example (11) below.

11. a. **Huan 'o 'am ki: ba:ṣo cipkan.**
    b. **Huan 'o 'am cipkan ki: ba:ṣo.**
    } John is/was working in front of the house.

The (b) sentence has a new word order; the postposition and the noun object are moved to the end of the sentence, but the specifier is left behind.

Huan	**'o**	**'am**	**ki:**	**ba:ṣo**	**cipkan.**
SUBJECT	AUX	SPECIFIER	OBJECT	POSTPOSITION	VERB

Huan	**'o**	**'am**	**cipkan**	**ki:**	**ba:so.**
SUBJECT	AUX	SPECIFIER	VERB	OBJECT	POSTPOSITION

The sentence in example (12), which has a postpositional phrase with a pronoun object, has the same order possibilities.

12. a. **Mali:ya ’o ’am ñ-ba’ic dahă.**
    b. **Mali:ya ’o ’am dahă ñ-ba’ic.**
    Mary is/was sitting in front of me.

Here are some more examples of sentences with postpositional phrases.

13. a. **Hegam ’o’odham ’o ’am do’ag we:big ki:.**
    b. **Hegam ’o’odham ’o ’am ki: do’ag we:big.**
    Those people are/were living behind the mountain.

14. a. **’Ali ’o ’an wo’ikuḍ da:m wo’o kc ko:ṣ.**
    b. **Ali ’o ’an wo’o kc ko:ṣ wo’ikuḍ da:m.**
    The child is/was lying on the bed and sleeping.

15. a. **Husi ’o ’am m-we:big ke:k.**
    b. **Husi ’o ’am ke:k m-we:big.**
    Joe is/was standing behind you.

16. a. **Gogs ’o ’an ha-hugidan wo’o.**
    b. **Gogs ’o ’an wo’o ha-hugidan.**
    The dog is/was lying next to him (her, it).

17. a. **Mimstol ’o ’an ma:gina da:m daḍhă.**
    b. **Mimstol ’o ’an daḍhă ma:gina da:m.**
    The cats are/were sitting on top of the car.

18. a. **Ju:kĭ ’o ’ab t-wui him.**
    b. **Ju:kĭ ’o ’ab him t-wui.**
    The rain is coming (*literally* walking) toward us.

19. a. **’U’uwĭ ’o’am kui weco daḍhă kc ñeñok.**
    b. **’U’uwĭ ’o ’am daḍhă kc ñeñok kui weco.**
    The women are/were sitting under the tree and talking.

20. a. **Huan ’o ’am ’em-wui him.**
    b. **Huan ’o ’am him ’em-wui.**
    John is/was walking toward you (*pl.*).

21. a. **Klisti:na ’o ’an ha-hugidan dahă hegam.**
    b. **Klisti:na ’o ’an dahă ha-hugidan hegam.**
    Christina is/was sitting next to them.

22. a. **Hegai kui ’o ’ab to:nk ba:ṣo ke:k.**
    b. **Hegai kui ’o ’ab ke:k to:nk ba:ṣo.**
    That tree is/was standing in front of (at the base of) the hill.

LOCATIVES

The term *locative* refers to the members of the list of location words given below. Note that there are two forms for each locative—a long form and a short form.

Long Form	*Short Form*	*Translation*
'amai	**'am**	over there (*in front of speaker*)
'anai	**'an**	over there (*next to speaker*)
gaḍhu	**gḍhu**	over there (*out of sight of speaker*)
ganhu	**gnhu**	over there (*in sight of speaker*)
'eḍa	**'eḍ**	inside, in
'i:ma	**'im**	back here, there (*in back of speaker*)
'i:ya	**'i**	right here

A locative simply gives the location of some object, as shown in the following examples.

23. a. **Mali:ya 'o 'i:ya dahă.**
    b. **'I:ya 'o dahă g Mali:ya.** } Mary is/was sitting right here.
24. a. **Klisti:na 'o 'amai 'oimeḍ.**
    b. **'Amai 'o 'oimeḍ g Klisti:na.** } Christina is/was walking around over there.
25. a. **Husi 'o 'anai ke:k ki: hugidan.**
    b. **'Anai 'o ke:k g Husi ki: hugidan.** } Joe is/was standing over there next to the house.
26. a. **'A'al 'o 'i:ma cicwi ñ-we:big.**
    b. **'I:ma 'o cicwi ñ-we:big g 'a'al.** } The children are/were playing behind me.
27. a. **Hegam 'o gaḍhu dadhă ki: eḍa.**
    b. **Gaḍhu 'o daḍhă ki: eḍa hegam.** } They are/were sitting in the house.

In most cases the shorter form of the locative can be substituted for the longer form.

28. a. **'I 'o dahă g Mali:ya.** Mary is/was sitting right here.
    (*The locative 'i can occur only in initial position.*)
29. a. **Klisti:na 'o 'am 'oimed.**
    b. **'Am 'o 'oimed g Klisti:na.** } Christina is/was walking around over there.
30. a. **Husi 'o 'an ke:k.**
    b. **'An 'o ke:k g Husi.** } Joe is/was standing over there.

31. a. **'Im 'o cicwi g 'a'al.** } The children are/were playing
    b. **'A'al 'o 'im cicwi.** } back here.

32. a. **Hegam 'o gḍhu daḍhă.** } They are/were sitting over
    b. **Gḍhu 'o daḍhă hegam.** } there.

NOTE: The short locative form 'i must be in the initial position of the sentence in which it occurs.

EXERCISES

A. Answer the following questions in Papago using both the postpositional phrases and the locatives which were introduced in this lesson.

1. Where do you live?
2. Where do you work?
3. What is John walking toward?
4. Who was standing in front of Mary?
5. Where is the dog lying?
6. What is John sitting next to?
7. Where was Joe going?
8. Where is Mary sleeping?
9. Where are the children playing?
10. What is the cat lying on (on top of)?
11. Where does Joe live?
12. What is Christina sitting next to?

B. Translate the following sentences:

1. **Mali:ya 'o 'ab t-wui him.**
2. **Mi:stol 'o 'am ma:gina weco wo'o kc ko:s.**
3. The women were standing over here.
4. She's standing over here.
5. Joe is lying on the bed and writing something.
6. **Husi 'o gaḍhu cipkan to:nk we:big.**
7. Those women are sitting over there under the tree.
8. John was lying under the tree and sleeping.
9. **Hegam 'a'al 'o 'am ki: we:big daḍhă kc cicwi.**
10. **Ṣu:dagĭ 'o 'an meḍ do'ag hugidan.**
11. He's sitting over there.
12. He's standing right here next to you.

LESSON 9

Interrogative Sentences
Who (Whom), What, and *Where* Questions

VOCABULARY

NOUNS

Singular	*Plural*
pi ha'icu nothing *(concrete)*	—
pi has nothing *(abstract)*	—
pi heḍai nobody, no one	—

VERBS

'elid thinking *(reflexive)*	**'elid** thinking
hihidoḍ cooking	**hihidoḍ** cooking
kaij saying	**kaij** saying
wua doing *(reflexive)*	**wua** doing

OTHER EXPRESSIONS

pi hebai nowhere
we:m with

PRE-AUXILIARY QUESTION WORDS

The following sentences are examples of *who* (*whom*), *what*, and *where* questions in Papago:

1. **Ṣa: 'o kaij g Huan?** What is/was John saying?
2. **Ṣa:cu 'o ñu:kud g Huan?** What is/was John taking care of?
3. **Do: 'o kuḍut g 'ali?** Who is/was bothering the baby?
4. **Ba: 'o 'oimed g gogs?** Where is/was the dog walking around?

In all of these examples the question word begins the sentence and directly precedes the auxiliary. The table below gives the pre-auxiliary forms of these question words:

do:	who, whom
ṣa:	what *(abstract)*
ṣa:cu	what *(concrete)*
ba:	where

The following are more examples of the pre-auxiliary forms of *who*, (*whom*), *what*, and *where* questions:

5. **Ṣa: 'o kaij g cehia?** What is/was the girl saying?
6. **Ṣa:cu 'o huhu'id g 'ali?** What is/was the child chasing?
7. **Do: 'o cipkan 'am ki: we:big?** Who is/was working behind the house?
8. **Ba: 'o cicwi g 'a'al?** Where are/were the children playing?
9. **Ṣa: p 'e-wua 'a:pi?** / **Ṣa: p 'e-wua?** } What are/were you doing?
10. **Ṣa: ñ ñ-wua 'a:ñi?** / **Ṣa: ñ ñ-wua?** } What am/was I doing?
11. **Ṣa: c t-wua 'a:cim?** / **Ṣa: c t-wua?** } What are/were we doing?
12. **Ṣa: m 'e-wua 'a:pim?** / **Ṣa: m 'e-wua?** } What are/were you (*pl.*) doing?
13. **Ṣa:cu 'ap ñeid 'a:pi?** / **Ṣa:cu 'ap ñeid?** } What are/were you seeing (looking at)?
14. **Ṣa:cu 'o da:m dahă g ceoj?** What is/was the boy sitting on top of?
15. **Do: 'o ṣoak?** Who is/was crying?
16. **Do: 'o ñu:kud g 'ali?** Who is/was taking care of the baby?
17. **Ba: 'o 'oimeḍ g 'uwĭ?** Where is/was the girl walking around?
18. **Ba: 'o cipkan g ceoj?** Where is/was the boy working?

POST-AUXILIARY QUESTION WORDS

Question words in interrogative sentences can also occur in post-auxiliary position, but when they do, they have different forms. The table below shows the post-auxiliary forms for question words:

heḍai	who, whom
has	what (*abstract*)
hascu	what (*concrete*)
hebai	where

Listed below are examples of interrogative sentences in which the question word follows a special form of the imperfective auxiliary:

19. **Ñ has ñ-wua?** What am/was I doing?
20. **P hascu hihidod?** What are/were you cooking?
21. **K heḍai ṣoak?** Who is/was crying?
22. **M hebai cickpan 'a:pim?** Where do you (*pl.*) work?

Some speakers add the prefix **ku** to the special form of the auxiliary for the first and second persons in the post-auxiliary question form, as in the following examples:

23. **Kup has 'e-wua?** What are/were you doing?
24. **Kum hebai 'oyopo 'a:pim?** Where are/were you (*pl.*) walking?
25. **Kuc heḍai 'am huhu'id?** Whom are/were we chasing?
26. **Kum hascu hihidod 'a:pim?** What are/were you (*pl.*) cooking?

Note that in examples 19–26 the initial auxiliaries have the same forms as those first introduced in Lesson 5 on conjunctions. These special forms of the auxiliary are listed below:

Singular		*Plural*	
SHORT FORM	LONG FORM*	SHORT FORM	LONG FORM*
ñ	**kuñ**	**c**	**kuc**
p	**kup**	**m**	**kum**
k	—	**k**	—

*Rarely used.

NOTE: When the post-auxiliary form is used, it directly follows the auxiliary, which for these questions moves to initial position in the sentence.

The following are more examples of the post-auxiliary forms of *who* (*whom*), *what*, and *where* questions:

27. **K has 'e-wua g cehia?** What is/was the girl doing?
28. **K has kaij g Husi?** What does/did Joe say?
29. **K hascu ñu:kud g cehia?** What is/was the girl taking care of?
30. **K hascu kuḍut g 'ali?** What is/was the child bothering?
31. **K heḍai 'an mi:sa da:m dahă?** Who is/was sitting on top of the table?
32. **K heḍai hehem?** Who is/was laughing?
33. **Kum heḍai huhu'id 'a:pim?** Whom are/were you (*pl.*) chasing?
34. **K hebai cicwi g 'ali?** Where is/was the child playing?
35. **Kup hebai ke:k 'a:pi?** Where are/were you standing?
36. **Kum hebai 'oyopo 'a:pim?** Where are/were you (*pl.*) walking around?

QUESTIONS WITH AMBIGUOUS MEANINGS

The questions listed below are ambiguous in the sense that the question form can be interpreted either as the subject or as the direct object of the sentence. (The ambiguity does not carry over into English, because the subject "who" has a different form—"whom"—as the direct object and because of the sentence word order.)

37. **Do: 'o kuḍut g 'ali?** { Who is/was bothering the baby? / Whom is/was the baby bothering?
38. **Do: 'o dagkon g cehia?** { Who is/was drying the girl? / Whom is/was the girl drying?
39. **Do: 'o huhu'id g gogs?** { Who is/was chasing the dog? / Whom is/was the dog chasing?

40. **K hascu huhu'id ceoj?** { What is/was the boy chasing? What is/was chasing the boy?

41. **K heḍai kuḍut g cehia?** { Who is/was bothering the girl? Whom is/was the girl bothering?

SOME USEFUL QUESTIONS IN PAPAGO

42. **K hebai ke:k g tianda?** Where is the store? (*Literal:* Where is the store standing? *Use the verb* **ke:k** [standing] *to ask where a building is located.*)
43. **K hebai ki: g Huan?** Where does John live?
44. **Ba: pt o hi:?** Where are you going?
45. **Ṣa: p kaij?** What did you say? (*Can also be used as a general greeting*)
46. **Ṣa: p 'a'i masma?** How have you been? (*General greeting*)
47. **Ṣa: p-'e-wua?** What are you doing? (*General greeting*)
48. **P hebai ki:?** Where do you live?
49. **Ṣa: p 'a'aga 'i:da?** What do you call this?
50. **Ṣa:cu 'o ḍ 'i:da?** What is this thing?
51. **Do: 'o ḍ hegai?** Who is that (he, she)?

NOTE: Some questions can be answered with the words *nobody* or *no one, nothing,* or *nowhere.* To form these words, in general simply put the negative word **pi** in front of the appropriate post-auxiliary question word:

pi heḍai	nobody, no one
pi has	nothing (*abstract*)
pi hebai	nowhere

However, the Papago word for *nothing* (concrete) is not ***pi hascu.** Instead **pi** is added to **ha'icu** 'thing.'

pi ha'icu nothing (*concrete*)

EXERCISES

A. Translate the following questions into Papago using either pre-aux or post-aux question word forms:

1. Where does Maria live?
2. What does Joe see?
3. What is John saying?
4. Who is bothering you?
5. What are you cooking?
6. What were the children doing?
7. Who was taking care of the children?
8. What is Joe doing?

B. Answer the following questions in Papago:

1. Ba: p ki:?
2. Kup hebai cipkan?
3. Ṣa:cu 'ap 'ab cipkan?
4. Do: 'o m-we:m cipkan?
5. Ṣa: 'o 'e-wua g Piwulu?
6. K hebai dahă g Piwulu?
7. K heḍai 'am cicwi ki: webig?
8. Do: 'o ab meḍ m-wui?

C. *For native speakers only.* Translate the following Papago statements. The statements all contain some form of question words, but their meaning is not as clear as in the previous questions you have been looking at. Try to translate these statements into English as closely as you can. If necessary, give instances in which you would use these statements:

1. Hegai 'o ge has kaij.
2. Hegai 'o ge has 'e-elid.
3. Hascu 'a:gĭ?
4. Hebai hasko?
5. Kutp heḍai hab 'i 'a:gĭ.
6. Ṣa: p 'a'i masma?
7. Hebai na'a.

Perfective and Future Perfective Verbs

VOCABULARY

NOUNS

Singular		*Plural*	
cu:hug, cu:kug	meat	**cu:hug, cu:kug**	meats
hodai	rock, stone	**hohodai**	rocks, stones
pualt	door	**pupualt**	doors
ṣa'i	hay, grass	**ṣa'i**	hay, grass
waṣai	grass, hay	**waṣai**	grasses

VERBS

o'oha (*perf.*)	wrote	**'o'oha** (*perf.*)	wrote
ṣonwui (*perf.*)	pounded	**ṣonwui** (*perf.*)	pounded

PERFECTIVE VERB FORMS—COMPLETED ACTION

So far we have used only the verb form which indicates ongoing action in the present or past (the *imperfective*). In this lesson we will introduce the form which indicates completed action (the *perfective*). Listed below are the perfective forms for some verbs you have already seen in the imperfective:

Imperfective			*Perfective*		
Singular		*Plural*	*Singular*		*Plural*
him	walking	**hihim**	**hi:**	walked	**hihi**
hi:nk	barking	**hihink**	**hi:n**	barked	**hihin**
huhu'id	chasing	**huhu'id**	**huhu'i**	chased	**huhu'i**
meḍ	running	**wo:po'ŏ**	**me:**	ran	**wo:p**
ñeid	seeing	**ñeid**	**ñei**	saw	**ñei**
ñeok	speaking	**ñeñok**	**ñeo**	spoke	**ñeñeo**

In most cases the perfective can be derived from the imperfective by dropping the final consonant of the imperfective for both singular and plural forms.

Imperfective	*Perfective*
hi*m*	**hi:**
hihin*k*	**hihin**
huhu'i*d*	**huhu'i**
me*ḍ*	**me:**
ñei*d*	**ñei**
ñeo*k*	**ñeo**

The following is a list of new verbs, in both the imperfective and perfective forms. These verbs form the perfective in the regular fashion.

Imperfective			*Perfective*		
Singular		*Plural*	*Singular*		*Plural*
ce'ewid	covering	**ce'ewid**	**ce'ewi**	covered	**ce'ewi**
golon	raking	**golon**	**golo**	raked	**golo**
he:lwuin	sliding	**hehelwuin**	**he:lwui**	slid	**hehelwui**
'o'ohan	writing	**'o'ohan**	**'o'oha**	wrote	**'o'oha**
si:ṣp	pinning, nailing	**sisiṣp**	**si:ṣ**	pinned, nailed	**sisiṣ**
ṣonwuin	hitting, pounding	**ṣonwuin**	**ṣonwui**	hit, pounded	**ṣonwui**
woson	sweeping	**woson**	**woso**	swept	**woso**

However, not all verbs are quite so regular. Some verbs drop more than the final consonant from the imperfective to form the perfective—the final vowel and consonant are dropped:

Imperfective		*Perfective*	
cepos*id*	branding	**cepos**	branded
cipk*an*	working	**cipk**	worked
gegos*id*	feeding	**gegos**	fed

In at least one verb, the final vowel, consonant, and vowel are dropped:

Imperfective		*Perfective*	
wo:po'ŏ	running (*pl.*)	**wo:p**	ran (*pl.*)

For other verbs, there is no change at all:

Imperfective		*Perfective*	
cicwi	playing	**cicwi**	played
gagswua	combing	**gagswua**	combed
ka:	hearing	**ka:**	heard

And then there are some verbs for which the change is very irregular:

Imperfective			*Perfective*		
Singular		*Plural*	*Singular*		*Plural*
ju:k	raining	—	**ju:**	rained	—
ko'a	eating	**ko'a**	**hu:**	ate	**hu:**
ko:ṣ	sleeping	**ko:kṣ**	**koi**	slept	**ko:k**
meḍ	running	**wo:po'o**	**me:**	ran	**wo:p**
na:d	making a fire	—	**nai**	made a fire	**nai**
si'i	sucking	**si'i**	**si:**	sucked	**si:**
wo'o	lying down	**wo:p**	**woi**	lay down	**woi**
wupḍa	roping, tying	**wupḍa**	**wu:**	roped, tied	**wu:**

THE PERFECTIVE AUXILIARY

Now that you know how to make the perfective form of a verb, compare the following two sentences. The first sentence has an imperfective verb; the second has a perfective verb.

'A:ñi ***'añ*** **ñeok.** I am/was speaking.

'A:ñi ***'ant*** **ñeo.** I spoke.

Note that the auxiliary in the first sentence is different from that in the second sentence. With the perfective form of the verb, the auxiliary contains **t**. The chart below gives the perfective forms of the auxiliary; each contains **t**.

	Singular		*Plural*	
	LONG FORM	SHORT FORM	LONG FORM	SHORT FORM
1st person	**'ant**	**nt**	**'att**	**tt**
2nd person	**'apt**	**pt**	**'amt**	**mt**
3rd person	**'at**	**t**	**'at**	**t**

You know the imperfective forms of the auxiliary, but they are given again below for comparison with the perfective forms.

	Singular		*Plural*	
	LONG FORM	SHORT FORM	LONG FORM	SHORT FORM
1st person	**'añ**	**ñ**	**'ac**	**c**
2nd person	**'ap**	**p̣**	**'am**	**m**
3rd person	**'o**	**'o**	**'o**	**'o**

Examples of imperfective and perfective sentences:

1. a. **Ceoj *'o* ñeok.** The boy is/was speaking.
   b. **Ceoj *'at* ñeo.** The boy spoke.
2. a. **'Uwĭ *'o* ñeid g ceoj.** The woman sees the boy.
   b. **'Uwĭ *'at* ñei g ceoj.** The woman saw the boy.
3. a. **'A:pi *'ap* him 'am ki: wui.** You are/were walking to the house.
   b. **'A:pi *'apt* hi: 'am ki: wui.** You walked to the house.
4. a. **'A:cim *'ac* cicpkan 'am ki: webig.** We are/were working behind the house.
   b. **'A:cim *'att* cicpk 'am ki: webig.** We worked behind the house.
5. a. **'A:pim 'am wo:po'ŏ 'am tianda wui.** You (*pl.*) are/were running to the store.
   b. **'A:pim *'amt* wo:p 'am tianda wui.** You (*pl.*) ran to the store.

The following are more examples of sentences with perfective verbs:

6. **Mali:ya 'at woso g ki:.** Maria swept the house.
7. **'Ali 'at 'i-helwui 'ab hodai 'amjed.** The child slid down from the rock.
8. **Klisti:na 'at ṣoñwui g cu:hug.** Christina pounded the meat.
9. **Cehia 'at ha'icu 'o'oha.** The girl wrote something.
10. **Golo 'at g ṣa'i g Huan.** John raked the grass.
11. **Hegai 'at e-ce'ewi.** He covered himself.
12. **Hegai 'at si:ṣ g pualt.** He nailed the door.

THE FUTURE PERFECTIVE

One way to express future time in Papago is to add **o** before the perfective form of the verb:

Ceoj 'at ñeo. The man spoke.

Ceoj at *o* ñeo. The man will speak.

The future marker **o** is quite different from the imperfective auxiliary **'o**. The future **o**, which does not have a glottal stop, occurs only with perfective verbs and it always comes immediately before the verb:

Wakial	**'o**	**g wisilo**	**ceposid.**	The cowboy is/was branding the calf.
	AUX		IMPERFECTIVE	

Wakial	**'at**	**g wisilo**	**o**	**cepos.**	The cowboy will brand the calf.
	AUX		FUTURE MARKER	PERFECTIVE	

Sentences illustrating the future perfective are shown below:

13. a. **Ceoj 'at ñeo.** The boy spoke.
    b. **Ceoj 'at o ñeo.** The boy will speak.
14. a. **'Uwĭ 'at ñei g ceoj.** The woman saw the boy.
    b. **'Uwĭ 'at o ñei g ceoj.** The woman will see the boy.
15. a. **'A:pi 'apt hi: 'am ki: wui.** You walked to the house.
    b. **'A:pi 'apt o hi: 'am ki: wui.** You will walk to the house.
16. a. **'A:cim 'att hihi 'am tianda wui.** We walked to the store.
    b. **'A:cim 'att o hihi 'am tianda wui.** We will walk to the store.
17. a. **Hegai 'uwĭ 'at woso g ki:.** That woman swept the house.
    b. **Hegai 'uwĭ 'at o woso g ki:.** That woman will sweep the house.
18. a. **Husi 'at ha'icu 'o'oha.** Joe wrote something.
    b. **Ha'icu 'at o 'o'oha g Husi.** Joe will write something.
19. a. **Wakial 'at golo g waṣai.** The cowboy raked the hay.
    b. **Wakial 'at o golo g waṣai.** The cowboy will rake the hay.
20. a. **Klisti:na 'at 'e-ce'ewi.** Christina covered herself.
    b. **Klisti:na 'at o 'e-ce'ewi.** Christina will cover herself.

EXERCISES

A. Give the (a) perfective form and (b) future perfective form of the following sentences:

1. 'I:da 'o'odham 'o ñeok.
2. Hegai 'uwĭ 'o cipkan.
3. 'Idam cecoj 'o ñeñok.
4. Hegai cehia 'o cicwi.
5. Haiwañ 'o him.
6. Mi:stol 'o si'i.
7. Hegai ceoj 'o na:d.
8. Ju:k 'o.

B. Translate the following questions into English:

1. Nat ko:k g 'a'al?
2. Napt cipk 'a:pi?
3. Napt o cipk 'a:pi?
4. Natt 'a:cim 'am o hihi tianda wui?
5. Nat g Mali:ya woso g ki:?
6. Napt 'a:pi 'e-eñigadad?
7. Natt 'am o wo:p Cuk Ṣon wui?
8. Nat ju:?

C. Give the (a) perfective and (b) future perfective forms for the following sentences in Papago:

1. The woman is/was bothering us.
2. That child is/was bothering us.
3. That girl is/was taking care of you (*pl.*).
4. The child is/was playing under the table.
5. The calf is/was running.
8. Is/was the cow sleeping?
9. Is/was Maria walking toward you?
10. Are the children playing?

First Review Lesson

VOCABULARY

Translate the following words into Papago:

1. working
2. speaking
3. girl
4. woman
5. boy
6. person
7. dog
8. horses
9. cows
10. calves
11. cat
12. running (*sg.*)
13. walking (*pl.*)
14. barking (*sg.*)
15. sleeping (*sg.*)
16. cowboys
17. rabbit
18. table
19. house
20. chair
21. coyote
22. cars
23. speaking (*pl.*)
24. taking care of (*sg.*)
25. herding (*sg.*)
26. branding (*pl.*)
27. seeing (*sg.*)
28. chasing (*pl.*)
29. shooting (*sg.*)
30. hearing (*sg.*)
31. washing
32. feeding
33. warming
34. scratching
35. kicking
36. cutting
37. wiping
38. putting clothes on
39. combing (*sg.*)
40. saying (*sg.*)

PRONOUNS AND AUXILIARIES

1. List the imperfective personal pronouns and their auxiliaries.
2. List all of the reflexive prefix forms for Papago.
3. Give both the pre-auxiliary form and the post-auxiliary forms for *who, what* (abstract and concrete), and *where* in Papago.

NEGATIVE SENTENCES

Change the following statements into negative sentences:

1. Soañ 'o 'idam 'a'al.
2. Hegam gogogs 'o ko:kṣ.
3. Jerry 'o ṣoak.
4. Klisti:na 'o cicwi.
5. Nellie 'o cipkan.
6. 'Anto:n 'o ceposid g haiwañ.

CONJOINED SENTENCES

Translate the following conjoined sentences into English:

1. Travis 'o cipkan kuñ 'a:ñi ko:ṣ.
2. Jerry 'o ñeok kup 'a:pi cicwi.
3. 'A'al 'o cicwi kuc 'a:cim cicpkan.
4. 'U'uwĭ 'o wo:po'ŏ kum 'a:pim hihim.

DIRECT AND INDIRECT OBJECTS

Translate the following sentences:

1. Earl 'o ha-huhu'id g totobĭ.
2. Nellie 'o ha-ñu:kud g 'a'al.
3. Klisti:na 'o ha-ṣa:mud g wipsilo.
4. John is taking care of the cows for Joe.
5. No ha-ñeid g ki:k g Husi?
6. Pi'a, pi 'o ha-ñeid g ki:k g Husi.

7. John was giving calves to the people.
8. Nap 'a:pi g haiwañ ceposid hegai ceoj we:hejeḍ?
9. Huan we:hejeḍ 'ac ha-kegcid g dadaikuḍ.

WORD ORDER

Translate the following sentences into Papago and give both possible word orders:

1. I am working.
2. You are/were playing.
3. He (she, it) is/was sleeping.
4. We are/were chasing the cat.
5. You (*pl.*) are/were washing yourselves.
6. They are/were combing themselves (their hair).

GRAMMAR RULES

1. Explain the rule concerning the position of the Papago auxiliary (except the special form of the auxiliary used in conjoined sentences and in some *who, what,* and *where* questions). Give five sentences illustrating the rule. If possible, use some original sentences. Now, explain how the special form of the auxiliary used in conjoined sentences and in *who, what,* and *where* questions is different.

2. Give the rule about the determiner 'g.' Illustrate this rule with at least five original sentences.

POSTPOSITIONAL PHRASES

Use the following post-positional phrases in some original sentences:

1. 'an . . . da:m
2. 'am . . . weco
3. 'ab . . . wui
4. 'am . . . wui
5. 'ab . . . ba:ṣo

PART II
Second Grammar Unit

LESSON 11

Future Imperfective Verbs

VOCABULARY

NOUNS

Singular		*Plural*	
ke:li	man, old man	**kekel**	men, old men
mo'o	hair	**mo'o**	hairs
sigal	cigarette	**sigal**	cigarettes

VERBS

'i:'e	drinking	**'i:'e**	drinking
je:ñ	smoking	**je:ñ**	smoking

FORMATION OF THE FUTURE IMPERFECTIVE

In Lesson 10 you learned how to form the future perfective. There is another form to express the future—the future imperfective. To form the future imperfective of a verb, add **ad** to the imperfective verb form:

Imperfective		*Future Imperfective*	
ñeok	is/was speaking	**ñeokad**	will be speaking
meḍ	is/was running	**meḍad**	will be running

Simply add **d** if the imperfective verb ends in a vowel:

Imperfective		*Future Imperfective*	
ñe'e	is/was singing	**ñe'ed**	will be singing
cicwi	is/was playing	**cicwid**	will be playing

The plural forms of the future imperfective are the same as the plural imperfective forms, with **ad** or **d** added.

Plural Imperfective		*Plural Future Imperfective*	
cicwi	playing	**cicwid**	will be playing
ñeñok	speaking	**ñeñokad**	will be speaking
'oyopo	walking around	**'oyopod**	will be walking around
wo:po'ŏ	running	**wo:po'od**	will be running

COMPARISON OF THE FUTURE IMPERFECTIVE AND THE FUTURE PERFECTIVE

With the future imperfective use the same auxiliary form as with the future perfective and also include the future particle **o.** Compare the following:

Ceoj 'o ñeok. The boy is/was speaking.

Ceoj 'at ñeo. The boy spoke.

Ceoj 'at o ñeo. The boy will speak.

Ceoj 'at o ñeokad. The boy will be speaking.

The following are examples of sentences in the future imperfective.

1. a. **Napt 'i:ya o cipkanad?** Will you be working here?
   b. **Namt 'i:ya o cicpkanad 'a:pim?** Will you (*pl.*) be working here?
2. a. **Hegai 'ali 'at o si ṣoakad.** That child will really be crying.
   b. **Hegam 'a'al at o si ṣoañad.** Those children will really be crying.
3. a. **Hegai ke:li 'at o si ñe'ed.** That old man will really be singing.
   b. **Hegam kekel 'at o si ñeñed.** Those old men will really be singing.
4. a. **Ganhu 'at o himad g Huan.** John will be walking over there.
   b. **Ganhu 'at 'o hihimad hegam.** Those (people) will be walking over there.

5. a. **Hegai o'odham 'at o je:ñad g sigal.** That person will be smoking the cigarettes.

   b. **Hegam o'odham 'at o je:ñad g sigal.** Those people will be smoking the cigarettes.

EXERCISES

A. Give the perfective, future perfective, and the future imperfective form for all the following verbs.

ñeok	ceposid	wapkon	wo'o
ñeñok	cecposid	gegosid	wua
ko:ṣ	ñeid	hukṣan	'oimeḍ
ko:kṣ	huhu'id	keihin	'oyopo
'i:'e	gatwid	hikck	ju:k
ñu:kud	ka:	dagkon	
ṣa:mud	wakon	gaswua	

B. List the other three tenses for each of the verbs in the sentences below. Make sure that you use the appropriate auxiliary form.

1. Ceoj 'o ñeok.
2. 'Uwĭ 'o cipkan.
3. Husi 'at ṣoṣa.
4. Hegai 'ali 'o 'i:ya ko:ṣ.
5. Ṣu:dagĭ 'at 'i: g Huan.
6. Mali:ya 'at o ha-ñu:kut g 'a'al.
7. Cehia 'o ha-ṣa:mud g cucul.
8. Wakial 'at o ha-cecposidad g hahaiwañ.
9. No m-ñeid hegai?
10. Hegam 'o ha-gagtwid g totobĭ.
11. Pi:wulu 'o ha'icu ka:.
12. Gogs 'o e-hukṣan.
13. Ju:k 'o.

LESSON 12

Possessives

VOCABULARY

NOUNS

Singular		*Plural*	
daikuḍ	chair	**dadaikuḍ**	chairs
ga:t	gun	**gagt**	guns
ha:l	squash	**ha:l**	squash
je'e	mother	**je:j**	mothers
jeweḍ	land	**jeweḍ**	lands
kahio	leg	**kakkio**	legs
li:wa	jacket	**lilwa**	jackets
maḍ	child (of woman)	**ma:maḍ**	children (of woman)
ma:gina	car	**mamgina**	cars
mu:ñ	bean; pot of (cooked) beans	**mu:ñ**	beans; pots of (cooked) beans
nawaṣ	pocket knife	**nanwaṣ**	pocket knives
nowǐ	hand	**no:nowǐ**	hands
'oksga	wife	**'o'oksga**	wives
'o'ohana	book	**o'ohana**	books
'o:gǐ	father	**'o:gǐ**	fathers
kamiṣ	shirt	**kakmiṣ**	shirts
kotoñ	shirt	**koktoñ**	shirts
ṣu:ṣk	shoe	**ṣu:ṣk**	shoes
ta:ḍ	foot	**ta:taḍ**	feet
we:nag	brother/sister	**wepnag**	brothers/sisters

OTHER EXPRESSIONS

hugidan next to
si'alim tomorrow

SIMPLE POSSESSIVE CONSTRUCTIONS

The following phrases are examples of possessive construction:

1. **ceoj kotoñ** the boy's shirt
   BOY SHIRT

2. **wakial ga:t** the cowboy's gun
   COWBOY GUN

3. **Huan nawaṣ** John's pocket knife
   JOHN POCKET KNIFE

4. **Husi we:nag** Joe's brother/sister
   JOE BROTHER/SISTER

This is the simplest form for a possessive construction. It is simply a sequence of two nouns, in which the first noun indicates the possessor and the second the possessed.

Noun *Noun*
POSSESSOR POSSESSED

NOTE: A possessive construction is preceded by the **g** determiner when it occurs in a sentence, unless it occurs initially.

The following are examples of sentences with simple possessive constructions:

5. a. **'Ali je'e 'at o cipk si'alim.**
   b. **Si'alim 'at o cipk g 'ali je'e.**
   } The child's mother will work tomorrow.

6. a. **Mali:ya nawaṣ 'o 'an wo'o mi:sa da:m.**
   b. **'An 'o wo'o mi:sa da:m g Mali:ya nawaṣ.**
   } Mary's pocket knife is lying on top of the table.

7. a. **Uwĭ ki: 'o 'am ke:k do'ag we:big.**
   b. **Am do'ag we:big 'o ke:k g 'uwĭ ki:.**
   } The woman's house is standing behind the mountain.

8. a. **Husi li:wa 'apt o wako.**
   b. **'A:pi 'apt o wako g Husi li:wa.**
   } You will wash Joe's jacket.

POSSESSIVE PRONOUNS

The following examples illustrate a second type of possessive construction:

9. **ñ-je'e** my mother
   MY-MOTHER

10. **m-'o:gĭ** your father
    YOUR-FATHER

11. **t-'o'ohana** our books
    OUR-BOOKS

12. **'em-no:nowĭ** your (*pl.*) hands
    YOUR (*pl.*)-HANDS

13. **ha-kakkio** their legs
    THEIR-LEGS

14. **kotoñ-ij** his (her) shirt
    SHIRT-HIS

When the possessor is a pronoun, the possessed noun has a pronoun affix. The following table lists them:

	Singular	*Plural*
1st person	**ñ** my	**t-** our
2nd person	**m-** your	**'em-** your
3rd person	**-ij,-j** his, her, its	**ha-** their

Notice that the possession marker for third person singular is a suffix. The suffix has the form **-ij** when the noun to which it is attached ends in a consonant; when the noun ends in a vowel, the suffix has the form **-j**. Some examples are:

su:ṣk-ij his (her, its) shoes
taḍ-ij his (her, its) foot
nowĭ-j his (her) hand
li:wa-j his (her) jacket

NOTE: In the orthographic convention used in this text, suffixes are attached directly to the base word—i.e., **nowij** (his/her hand) or **li:waj** (his/her jacket). When first introduced, as in the table above, a *suffix* will be shown with a hyphen, but the written form will never be separated from the word to which it attaches. A *prefix,* on the other hand, is always separated by a hyphen in the written form—i.e., **ñ-je'e** (my mother).

The following are examples of sentences with possessive pronoun construction:

15. a. **Ñ-we:nag 'o 'am dahă ki: we:big.**
    b. **Am 'o dahă g ñ-we:nag ki: we:big.**
    My brother is/was sitting behind the house.
16. **No cipkan g m-o:gĭ?** Is/was your father working?
17. a. **'Em-je:j 'o gḍhu daḍhă kc ñeñok.**
    b. **Gḍhu 'o daḍha kc ñeñok g 'em-je:j.**
    Your (*pl.*) mothers are/were sitting over there and talking.

NOTE: Possessive pronoun constructions, like possessive noun constructions, are preceded by the **g** determiner except when they occur initially in the sentence. Thus, an initial phrase like **ñ-we:nag** (my brother) becomes **g ñ-we:nag** (*literally,* the my brother) when its position changes in the sentence.

Sample sentences (18) through (22) show more possessive pronoun constructions:

18. a. **Ha-ma:maḍ 'o ṣoañ.**
    b. **Soañ 'o g ha-ma:maḍ.**
    Their children are/were crying.
19. a. **Ñ-kotoñ c ñ-li:wa 'ant o wako.**
    b. **'Ant o wako g ñ-kotoñ c ñ-li:wa.**
    I will (am going to) wash my shirt and my jacket.
20. a. **Maḍij 'o 'am dahă.**
    b. **'Am 'o dahă g maḍij.**
    Her child is/was sitting there.
21. a. **Ñ-o:gĭ 'o 'am wo'o kc ko:ṣ kui weco.**
    b. **Kui weco 'o wo'o kc ko:ṣ g ñ-o:gĭ.**
    My father is/was lying under the tree and sleeping.
22. a. **Je'ej 'at o hihido g mu:ñ.**
    b. **Mu:ñ 'at o hihido g je'ej.**
    His (her) mother will cook the pot of beans.

THE SUFFIX -GA

We have discussed two types of possessive constructions. In either type, the possessed noun *may* take the suffix **-ga**, as in the following examples:

23. **Husi jewedga** Joe's land
24. **Huan kawyuga** John's horse
25. **Mali:ya ha:lga** Mary's squash
26. **ñ-mi:stolga** my cat
27. **t-haiwañga** our cows, cattle

In fact, some nouns, when they occur in a possessive construction, *require* the suffix-ga—like those above—and some nouns do not take the suffix-**ga**—like the examples in (1) through (4) or (9) through (14).

The following is a list of nouns which take the suffix **-ga** when they are the possessed noun in a possessive construction. Some of these words have been introduced earlier; the new ones should be learned now.

DOMESTIC ANIMALS

Singular		*Plural*	
cucul	chicken	**cucul**	chickens
gogs	dog	**gogogs**	dogs
haiwañ	cow	**hahaiwañ**	cows
kawyu	horse	**kakawyu**	horses
ko:ji	pig	**kokji**	pigs
mi:stol	cat	**mimstol**	cats
mu:la	mule	**mumla**	mules
pa:do	duck	**papdo**	ducks
potal	bronc	**poptol**	broncs
to:lo	bull	**totlo**	bulls
towa	turkey	**totwa**	turkeys
wisilo	calf	**wipsilo**	calves
wu:lo	burro	**wuplo**	burros

DOMESTIC PLANTS

ba:bas potato	**ba:bas** potatoes
ha:l squash	**hahal** squash
hu:ñ corn	**huhuñ** corn
mu:ñ bean, pot of (cooked) beans	**mu:ñ** beans, pots of (cooked) beans
toki cotton	**toki** cotton

WILD PLANTS

'auppa tree, cottonwood tree	**'a'auppa** trees, cottonwoods
ha:ṣañ saguaro	**hahaṣañ** saguaros
kui mesquite tree	**kukui** mesquite trees
naw prickly pear	**naw** prickly pears

PEOPLE

ke:li husband, man	**kekel** husbands, men
'oks wife, woman	**'o'oks** wives, women

MISCELLANEOUS

hodai rock	**hohodai** rocks
jewed̥ land	**jewed̥** lands
ṣu:dagĭ water	—
'u:s stick	**'u'us** sticks
wi:b milk	—

The following list of nouns are ones which do *not* take the suffix **-ga.** These nouns consist of *inherently possessed* things, such as body parts and kinship terms, as well as nouns which are said to be *inalienably possessed,* such as clothing and utensils.

BODY PARTS

Singular	*Plural*
ciñ, ceñ mouth	**ci:ciñ, ce:ceñ** mouths
da:k nose	**da:dk** noses
kahio leg	**kakkio** legs
mo'o head, head of hair	**mo:mĭ** heads, heads of hair

BODY PARTS (*continued*)

Singular	*Plural*
na:k ear	**na:nk** ears
nowĭ hand	**no:nowĭ** hands
'o: back	**'o:** backs
taḍ foot	**ta:taḍ** feet
to:n knee	**to:ton** knees
wuhĭ eye	**wu:pui** eyes

CLOTHING

kamiṣ shirt	**kakmiṣ** shirts
kotoñ shirt	**koktoñ** shirts
li:wa jacket	**lilwa** jackets
ṣaliwĭ pair of pants	**ṣaṣliwĭ** pairs of pants
ṣu:ṣk shoe, pair of shoes	**ṣu:ṣk** shoes, pairs of shoes
wonam hat	**wopnam** hats

PEOPLE

'alidag child (*of a man*)	**'a'alidag** children (*of a man*)
je'e mother	**je:j** mothers
maḍ child (*of a woman*)	**ma:maḍ** children (*of a woman*)
'o:gĭ father	**'o'ogĭ** fathers
we:nag brother/sister	**wepnag** brothers/sisters

TOOLS/UTENSILS

cihil pair of scissors	**cihil** pairs of scissors
ha'a pot, bottle	**haha'a** pots, bottles
hoa basket	**hoha** baskets
huasa'a plate	**huasaha'a** plates
nawaṣ pocket knife	**nawaṣ** pocket knives
pa:la shovel	**papla** shovels

MISCELLANEOUS

'ispul stirrup	**'i'ispul** stirrups
ki: house	**ki:kĭ** houses
ma:gina car	**mamagina** cars
si:l saddle	**si:l** saddles

The following are more examples of sentences with possessive constructions:

28. a. **'Ali gogsga 'at koi 'am wo'ikuḍ weco.**
    b. **Wo'ikuḍ weco 'at koi g 'ali gogsga.**
    } The child's dog slept under the bed.

29. a. **'A'al ha-wisiloga 'o si ṣoak.**
    b. **Si 'o ṣoak g 'a'al ha-wisiloga.**
    } The children's calf is/was really crying.

30. a. **Mali:ya maḍ 'o 'am 'oimeḍ kui weco.**
    b. **Kui weco 'o 'oimeḍ g Mali:ya maḍ.**
    } Mary's child is walking around under the tree.

31. a. **'A'al ha-gogogsga 'at wo:p 'am ñ-ki: wui.**
    b. **Ñ-ki: wui 'at wo:p g 'a'al ha-gogogsga.**
    } The children's dogs ran to my house.

32. a. **Cehia mi:stolga 'at o 'i: g wi:b.**
    b. **Wi:b 'at o 'i: g cehia mi:stolga.**
    } The child's cat will drink milk.

33. a. **Husi ma:ginaga 'at pi me:.**
    b. **Pi 'at me: g Husi ma:ginaga.**
    } Joe's car did not run.

34. a. **Klisti:na mo'o 'ant o wako.**
    b. **'Ant o wako g Klisti:na mo'o.**
    } I will wash Christina's hair.

35. a. **Ñ-o:gĭ wonam 'o 'an wo'o m-kamiṣ hugidan.**
    b. **M-kamiṣ hugidan 'o wo'o g ñ-o:gĭ wonam.**
    } My father's hat is/was lying next to your shirt.

36. a. **Ñ-pa:la 'o 'am ke:k ki: ba:ṣo.**
    b. **Ki: ba:ṣo 'o ke:k g ñ-pa:la.**
    } My shovel is/was standing in front of the house.

QUESTIONS INVOLVING POSSESSION: *WHOSE . . . ?*

In Lesson 9 we discussed *who, what,* and *where* questions. To ask the question *"Whose . . . ?"*, simply use the *who* question word forms **do:** or **hedai** (pre-auxiliary and post-auxiliary forms, respectively) instead of a noun or pronoun possessor.

37. *question:*	**Do: 'o kotoñ 'an wo'o?**	Whose shirt is/was lying there?
answer:	**Husi kotoñ 'o 'an wo'o.**	Joe's shirt is/was lying there.
38. *question:*	**K heḍai je'e cipkan?**	Whose mother is/was working?
answer:	**A:ñ 'o g ñ-je'e cipkan.**	My mother is/was working.
39. *question:*	**K heḍai je'e 'am ki: ceḍ dahă?**	Whose mother is/was sitting in the house?
answer:	**M-je'e 'o 'am dahă ki: ceḍ.**	Your mother is/was sitting in the house.
40. *question:*	**Do: t gogsga gegos g Husi?**	Whose dog did Joe feed?
answer:	**T-gogsga 'at gegos g Husi.**	Joe fed our dog.
41. *question:*	**T heḍai maḍ koi?**	Whose child went to sleep/slept?
answer:	**Ñ-we:nag maḍ 'at koi.**	My sister's child went to sleep/slept?
42. *question:*	**Do: kawyuga huhu'id g gogogs?**	Whose horse are/were the dogs chasing?
answer:	**Huan kawyuga 'o huhu'id g gogogs.**	The dogs are/were chasing John's horse.
43. *question:*	**T heḍai we:nag ceggia g Husi?**	Whose brother fought Joe? (*Or*, Whose brother did Joe fight?)
answer:	**Ñ-we:nag 'at ceggia g Husi.**	My brother fought Joe. (*Or*, Joe fought my brother.)
44. *question:*	**Do: pt ma:gina o wako?**	Whose car will you (are you going to) wash?
answer:	**Ñ-o:gĭ ma:gina 'ant o wako.**	I will wash (am going to wash) my father's car.
45. *question:*	**Nt heḍai ma:gina o wako?**	Whose car shall (will) I wash?
answer:	**Ñ-o:gĭ magina 'apt o wako.**	You will wash my father's car.

EXERCISES

A. Compose eight sentences with possessive constructions using nouns which take **-ga.**

B. Translate the following sentences into English:

1. K heḍai ma:gina 'an meḍ?
2. Pi:wulu gogsga 'at huhu'i g Husi ma:gina.
3. Mali:ya ha:lga 'o 'an dahă wo'ikuḍ da:m.
4. Do: 'o mu:laga 'am 'oimeḍ jekkad?
5. Hu:lia maḍ 'at 'am me: 'em-ki: wui.
6. Ba: t hi: g ñ-keliga?
7. Mali:ya maḍ kamiṣ 'o 'an wo'o daikuḍ hugidan.
8. M-oksga 'o 'ab him.

Copular (Linking) Sentences With *Wuḍ*

VOCABULARY

NOUNS

Singular		*Plural*	
'Akimel 'O'odham	Pima person	**'A'Akimel 'O'odham**	Pima people
ba:b	grandfather on mother's side	**ba:bab**	grandfathers on mother's side
bit	mud	**bit**	mud
Ci:no	Oriental person	**Cicno**	Oriental persons
da:d	senior aunt on mother's side	**da:da'a**	senior aunts on mother's side
hajuñ	cousin	**hahajuñ**	cousins
hakit	junior uncle on father's side	**ha:kit**	junior uncles on father's side
hu'ul	grandmother on mother's side	**huhu'ul**	grandmothers on mother's side
je'es	senior uncle on mother's side	**je:jes**	senior uncles on mother's side
jisk	junior aunt on mother's side	**jijsi**	junior aunt on mother's side
Ju:kam	Mexican-American (*male*), Mexican	**Jujkam**	Mexican-Americans (*males*); Mexicans
ka:k	grandmother on father's side	**ka:ka'a**	grandmothers on father's side
ke:li	senior uncle on father's sisde; old man	**kekel**	senior uncles on father's side; old men
kownal	governor, official	**kokownal**	governors, officials
Milga:n	Anglo person	**Mimilga:n**	Anglos
'o:bĭ	non-Papago person	**o'obĭ**	non-Papago persons

'oks old woman	**o'oks** old women
'oksi senior aunt on father's side	**'o'oksi** senior aunts on father's side
pa:l priest	**papal** priests
S-Cukcu Black person	**S-Cuckcu** Blacks
Sinaḍ Mexican-American, Mexican (*fem.*)	**Sisnaḍ** Mexican-Americans, Mexicans (*fem.*)
tatal junior uncle on mother's side	**ta:tal** junior uncles on mother's side
Tohono O'odham Papago person	**Tohono 'O'odham** Papago people
wosk grandfather on father's side	**wopsk** grandfathers on father's side
wowoit junior aunt on father's side	**wo:poit, wopowit** junior aunts on father's side

OTHER EXPRESSIONS

ge'ej big	**ge'egḍaj** big

SIMPLE COPULAR (LINKING) SENTENCES

The characteristic feature of copular (linking) sentences in Papago is the presence of the word **wuḍ**, which can come either just before or just after the auxiliary. This combination of the linking word and the aux connects the subject noun (or pronoun) with another noun (or pronoun) that completes the meaning of the subject and is the same person (or thing) as the subject. There is no transfer of action from one person to another person (or thing) in these sentences. The following are examples of copular sentences:

1. **'A:ñi 'añ wuḍ maistla.** I am/was a teacher.
2. **'A:pi 'ap wuḍ makai.** You are/were a doctor.
3. **Mali:ya 'o wuḍ Sinaḍ.** Mary is/was a Mexican-American woman.

The word **wuḍ** has a short form **ḍ**. In most copular sentences, either form is possible.

4. a. **Huan ’o wuḍ ñ-we:nag.**
   b. **Huan ’o ḍ ñ-we:nag.**
   } John is/was my brother.

5. a. **Hegai Milga:n ’o wuḍ pa:l.**
   b. **Hegai Milga:n ’o ḍ pa:l.**
   } That Anglo man is/was a priest.

6. a. **Hegai Ju:kam ke:li ’o wuḍ makai.**
   b. **Hegai Ju:kam ke:li ’o ḍ makai.**
   } That Mexican-American man is/was a doctor.

7. a. **Hegai ’oks ’o wuḍ ñ-hu’ul.**
   b. **Hegai ’oks ’o ḍ ñ-hu’ul.**
   } That old lady is my grandmother.

8. a. **’A:ñi ’añ wuḍ ’O’odham.**
   b. **’A:ñi ’añ ḍ ’O’odham.**
   } I am a Papago. (*Or*, I am Papago.)

In all the preceding examples, **wuḍ** (or **ḍ**) immediately follows the aux. There is one other possible position for **wuḍ**— it can occur initially in the sentence. However, when **wuḍ** is initial, most speakers use the short form **ḍ**.

9. **Ḍ ’añ maistla ’a:ñi.** I am a teacher.
10. **Ḍ ’o Huan ’o:gĭ hegai ke:li.** That old man is John’s father.
11. **Ḍ ’o ñ-hu’ul hegai ’oks.** That old woman is my grandmother.
12. **Ḍ ’o m-hajuñ g Mali:ya.** Mary is your cousin.
13. **Ḍ ’o ’oks g Klisti:na.** Christina is an old lady.

WUḌ IN NEGATIVE SENTENCES

The position of **wuḍ** in negative sentences is slightly different than in the affirmative copular sentences we have just discussed. In negative sentences, **wuḍ** cannot occur initially. Rather **wuḍ** (or **ḍ**) occurs after the auxiliary or, if the negative directly follows the auxiliary, after the negative.

14. a. **Pi ’o ḍ makai g Huan.**
    b. **Huan ’o pi wuḍ makai.**
    } John is not a doctor.

15. a. **Pi ’ac wuḍ Jujkam ’a:cim.**
    b. **’A:cim ’ac pi wuḍ Jujkam.**
    } We are not Mexican-Americans.

16. a. **Pi 'o ḍ ñ-hidoḍ 'i:da.**
    b. **'I:da 'o pi wuḍ ñ-hidoḍ.** } This is/was not my cooking.

17. a. **Pi 'o ḍ ñ-je'e hegai.**
    b. **Hegai 'o pi ḍ ñ-je'e.** } That (she) is not my mother.

18. a. **Pi 'o ḍ t-gogsga hegai**
    b. **Hegai 'o pi wuḍ t-gogsga.** } It (that) is/was not our dog.

WUḌ IN QUESTIONS

As in negative sentences, **wuḍ** cannot occur initially in questions. In questions, **wuḍ** can occur directly after the auxiliary or, if the subject of the sentence directly follows the auxiliary, directly after the subject.

19. **No g Klisti:na wuḍ m-maḍ?** Is Christina your child?
20. **No ḍ m-ba:b g Husi?** Is Joe your grandfather?
21. **Nap 'a:pi wuḍ pa:l?** Are/were you a priest?
22. **No hegai ḍ ñ-wosk?** Is that (he) my grandfather?
23. **Nap 'a:pi ḍ Husi?** Are you Joe?

EXERCISES

A. Translate the following sentences into English:

1. No wuḍ ke:li g m-'o:gĭ?
2. Pi 'o wuḍ sa'i 'oks g ñ-je'e.
3. Klisti:na 'o wuḍ ñ-maḍ.
4. Hegai ke:li 'o wuḍ ñ-hakit.
5. No wuḍ pa:l hegai Milga:n ke:li?
6. Hegam 'o wuḍ m-hahajuñ.
7. Nap wuḍ Tohono 'O'odham 'a:pi?
8. Ḍ 'o S-cukcu g Dr. Martin Luther King.
9. Hegai 'oks 'o wuḍ ñ-jisk.
10. Jimmy Carter 'o wuḍ ge'e kownal.

B. Change the word order of the following sentences:

1. Geronimo 'o wuḍ 'O:bĭ.
2. Ḍ 'o Ju:kam g Cesar Chavez.
3. Hegam 'o wuḍ Cicno.
4. Ḍ 'o 'Akimel 'O'odham g Ira Hayes.
5. Mali:ya 'o wuḍ maistla.
6. Ḍ 'o kownal hegai 'uwĭ.
7. Klisti:na 'o wuḍ ñ-we:nag.
8. Ḍ 'o makai hegai Milga:n ke:li.

C. Give four questions containing **wuḍ** and four negative sentences also containing **wuḍ.**

Formation of Verbs From Nouns
The Suffixes -mad and -pig

VOCABULARY

NOUNS

Singular	*Plural*
'asugal sugar	**'asugal** sugars
cu:hug, cu:kug meat	**cu:hug, cu:kug** meats
cu'i flour	—
hi:wodag sore, scab	**hihiwodag** sores, scabs
huasa'a, huhasa'a dish	**huhasaha'a** dishes
i:wuk, i:wagǐ wild spinach, greens	**i:wuk, i:wagǐ** greens
kahio leg	**kakkio** legs
kawhi coffee	**kawhi** coffees
ko'okol chile	**ko'okol** chiles
ku:bs smoke, dust	—
kulañ medicine	**kuklañ** medicines
meihǐ fire	**meihǐ** fires
'oil oil	**'oil** oils
'on salt	**'on** salts
siswui spit	—
sitol syrup, honey	**sitol** syrups, honeys
ṣawoñ soap	**ṣawoñ** soaps
ta:lko powder, talc	**ta:lko** powders, talcs
'u:s wood, board	**'u'us** boards
wa:ga dough	—
wuhioṣa face	**wuphioṣa** faces

OTHER EXPRESSIONS

cem hekid always
hahawa then

NOUNS TO VERBS: THE SUFFIX **-MAD**

In Papago some words can be turned into other words by adding certain suffixes or endings to them. In this lesson we will be discussing two suffixes—the suffix **mad** and the suffix **pig.** Both are added to nouns to turn them into verbs. For example:

Noun		*Verb*	
'asugal	sugar	**'asugalmad**	adding sugar to, sugaring

Thus, the noun **'asugal** (sugar) becomes the verb **'asugalmad** (adding sugar to)

NOTE: The plurals of these verbs formed with **-mad** have the same form as the singular (e.g., **'A:ñi 'añ 'onmad g cu:hug** [I am adding salt to the meat]; **'A:cim 'ac 'onmad g cu:hug** [We are adding salt to the meat]).

The following is a list of nouns which can be turned into verbs by adding the ending **-mad.**

Noun		*Verb*	
cu'i	flour	**cu'imad**	adding flour to, flouring
ko'okol	chile	**ko'okolmad**	adding chile to
ku:bs	smoke, dust	**ku:bsmad**	making smoky, causing dust
'oil	oil	**'oilmad**	adding oil to, oiling
'on	salt	**'onmad**	adding salt to, salting
ṣawoñ	soap	**ṣawoñmad**	adding soap to, soaping, washing
sitol	honey, syrup	**sitolmad**	adding honey to
ta:lko	talc, powder	**ta:lkomad**	adding powder to, powdering

The meaning of the verb formed with **mad** is, as these examples illustrate, "doing something with a noun (essentially what one would characteristically do with the noun)." So, the verb **ṣawoñmad** (**ṣawoñ** [soap] plus **mad**) means "doing with soap what one would characteristically do with soap," that is, "soaping."

However, some verbs with **mad** do not have such a simple relationship with the noun from which they are formed. Consider the following:

Noun		*Verb*	
jeweḍ	dirt	**jeweḍmad**	getting dirty
kulañ	medicine	**kulañmad**	making well, curing
siswui	spit	**siswuimad**	spitting on something

In these examples the noun and the verb formed from it by adding **mad** are obviously related in meaning, but it's slightly less easy to state exactly what that relationship is.

NOTE: Unlike verbs that change their form from imperfective to perfective, the newly formed verb using the suffix **-mad** stays the same. The aux is the only part of the sentence which would show it as being a perfective verb.

Examples

A:ñi 'añ ṣawoñmad g ñ-mo'o. I am/was soaping my hair.

A:ñi 'ant ṣawoñmad g ñ-mo'o. I soaped my hair.

The following are example sentences using the verbs formed with **mad.**

1. **Klistina 'at jeweḍmad g ñ-kotoñ.** Christina got my shirt dirty.
2. **Hegai 'ali 'o ñ-siswuimad.** That baby is/was spitting on me.
3. **Makai 'at kulañmad g ceoj.** The doctor made the boy well.
4. **Mali:ya 'at ṣawoñmad g ñ-mo'o.** Mary soaped my hair.
5. **Huan 'o 'onmad g cu:hug c ko'a.** John is/was putting salt on the meat and eating it.
6. **Mali:ya 'at cu'imad g cu:hug.** Mary floured the meat.
7. **Sisi:lia 'o ko'okolmad g mu:ñ c ko'a.** Cecelia is/was adding chile to the beans and eating (them).
8. **Ta:lkomad 'añ g 'ali.** I am/was powdering the baby.
9. **Pi:wulu 'o cem hekid sitolmad g 'e-kawhi.** Peter is/was always adding honey to his coffee.
10. **'Anto:n 'o 'oilmad g ñ-ma:gina.** Tony is/was oiling my car.
11. **Hegai ma:gina 'at t-ku:bsmad.** That car made us dusty (got dust on us).
12. **Nap 'asugalmad g kawhi?** Are/were you adding sugar to the coffee?

The list shown above does not include all the nouns you can add **-mad** to. However, it must be made clear that it isn't possible to add **-mad** to all Papago nouns. For example, the noun **sudagĭ** (water) cannot be made into a verb by adding **-mad** (***sudagĭmad**). There already is a Papago verb **wa:** meaning "to water." Verbs cannot be formed from nouns by adding **-mad,** if there already is a verb which means what that verb would mean. Some examples which illustrate this point are:

Noun	*Noun + -mad*	*Verb Which Already Exists*
bid mud	*bitmad	**bidṣ** getting muddy
kanjul lamp	*kanjulmad	**wegid** lighting up (with a lamp)

EXERCISES USING **-MAD**

A. Translate the following sentences into Papago:

1. The baby got himself dirty.
2. Are you washing (soaping) the dishes?
3. Did you flour the dough?
4. Is the doctor making your leg well?
5. The fire made the house smoky.
6. Did you powder your face?
7. No, I was not putting sugar in my coffee.
8. Yesterday I put honey in my coffee.

B. As you may have noticed, many of the verbs formed with **-mad** are based on nouns borrowed from Spanish or English. The use of **-mad** with these nouns is to be expected because of our earlier observation that a verb formed with **-mad** is possible only when there is no verb already existing in Papago. Since the introduction of nouns like **'asugal** or **ta:lko** probably accompanied the introduction into Papago life of such things as sugar, powder, and the like, it is to be expected that there would be no already existing Papago verb for "to sugar" or "to powder."

Below are some borrowed nouns. Add **-mad** to the noun and give the meanings of the new verbs.

1. **ba:bas** potato
2. **siwol** onion
3. **palwum** perfume
4. **pimiando** pepper

NOUNS TO VERBS: THE SUFFIX -PIG

Another ending in Papago which can also turn some nouns into verbs is the suffix **-pig.** Example:

Noun		*Verb*	
'eḍa	entrails, insides	**'eḍapig**	gutting
'on	salt	**'onpig**	removing salt
wopo	fur	**wopopig**	removing fur from the skin of an animal

By the translation we can see that the suffix **-pig** has the meaning of "removing," as in removing fur, insides, salt, and so on.

-Pig can also be added to parts of a related word to form a verb. For example:

***cel*pig** scraping off
***'el*pig** peeling
***gi'i*pig** removing fat from animal carcass
***hag*pig** removing leaves
***huk*pig** picking off, picking at with fingernail
***'oḍ*pig** scraping off sand
***ṣon*pig** hitting off, removing by hitting, chipping by hitting

In these examples **-pig** is added to elements which are not words by themselves; that is, **'el, ha, 'oḍ** are not words. However, we can find these same pieces of words in other words with obviously related meanings. For example:

Verb	*Related Word*	
celpig	***cel*kon**	scraping
'elpig	***'el*idag**	skin, peel
hagpig	***ha:*hag**	leaves
hukpig	***huk*i**	scratched
'oḍpig	**'o'*oḍ***	sand

When **pig** is added to part of a *noun,* the translation is still "to remove something." For example:

gi'ipig removing fat
hagpig taking the leaves off
'oḍpig removing sand

When **pig** is added to part of a *verb*, the translation indicates the method of removing. For example:

celpig scraping off (removing by scraping)
hukpig removing by scratching, picking with fingernail
ṣonpig removing by hitting

NOTE: Verbs created by adding the suffix **-pig** form the perfective by dropping the final consonant of the imperfective form and shortening the *i* which then remains at the end of the word.

Examples

onpig	removing salt	**onpĭ**	removed salt
elpig	peeling	**elpĭ**	peeled
gi'ipig	removing fat	**gi'ipĭ**	removed fat

Example sentences with verbs made by adding **-pig** are shown below:

13. **Huan 'at wopopĭ g haiwañ 'elidag.** John removed the hair from the cowhide.
14. **Husi 'o 'eḍapig g ko:ji c kegcid g cu:hug.** Joe is/was taking the insides out of the pig and cleaning the meat.
15. **Nap 'elpig g nalaṣ g 'ali weheje ḍ?** Are you peeling the orange for the child?
16. **'A:pi 'ap hagpig g 'i:wuk c hahawa hihidoḍ.** You are removing the leaves from the greens and then cooking (them).

NOTE: Sentences containing collective, or mass, nouns—such as **mu:ñ** (beans) or **'i:wagĭ** (greens)—as the direct object do not take the plural marker **ha-** on the verb. For example, we say **Mali:ya 'o g mu:ñ kegcid** (Mary is/was cleaning the beans) and not ***Mali:ya 'o g mu:ñ ha-kegcid.** These words, which are plural in meaning but singular in construction, also require the use of a singular verb.

17. **Mali:ya 'at celpĭ g bit.** Maria scraped off the mud.
18. **Makai 'at kulañmad g ñ-hi:wodag.** The doctor made my infection well.
19. **Hegam cecoj 'o ṣonpig hegai ge'e hodai.** Those boys are/were hitting and chipping that big rock.
20. **Hegam 'u'uwĭ 'o gi'ipig g ko:ji cu:hug.** Those women are/were removing the fat from the pork (pig meat).

Notice that there is no sentence illustrating the use of **'onpig** or **'oḍpig.** These words are not in general use any more.

EXERCISES USING -PIG

A. Give the correct verb phrase which fits the definition.

1. is/was removing leaves
2. is/was removing salt
3. removed by scratching or picking at
4. removed the insides
5. removed by hitting
6. is/was removing by scraping
7. is/was removing sand (from)
8. removing fur
9. removing skin, peeling
10. removing fat

B. Translate the following sentences into Papago:

1. John was scraping the board.
2. Maria peeled the potatoes.
3. Are you picking at the mud on your dress?
4. I am removing the fur (hair) from the pig skin.
5. Are you removing the fat from the pork (pig meat)?

LESSON 15

Formation of Nouns From Verbs

VOCABULARY

NOUNS

Singular	*Plural*
hewel wind	—
lial money	—

VERBS

golon raking	**golon** raking
hekaj *perf.* used	**hekaj** *perf.* used
kuint counting	**kukuint** counting
nolawt buying	**nolawt** buying
pa:nt making bread	**papant** making bread
pikcult taking a picture	**pipikcult** taking a picture
pisalt weighing	**pisalt** weighing
wakon washing	**wapkon** washing
woson sweeping	**woson** sweeping
wupḍa tying up	**wupḍa** tying up

THE NOUN AS A MODIFIED FORM OF THE IMPERFECTIVE

There are two ways to form a noun from a verb, but both of them depend on first changing the verb in one respect. That is, while **-mad** and **-pig** are attached directly to a noun to make a verb, in the cases which we will discuss here, the affixes indicating that the word is a noun are not added to the simple verb, but rather to a modified form of the verb.

Consider the following:

Verb		*Noun*	
woson	sweeping	a. **ñ-wosona**	the thing I swept, *or* my sweeping
		b. **wosonakuḍ**	instrument used to sweep with; a broom

In the second column above are two nouns formed from the verb in the first column. The two nouns are different in that one has a possessive prefix and the other has the suffix **-kuḍ.** But if we remove either of these two affixes, we see that they are attached to a form **wosona,** that is, the verb in the first column plus a suffix **-a.**

ñ- woson -a

woson -a - kuḍ

NOTE: Nouns formed by adding both the **-a** and the **-kuḍ** suffixes—such as **wosonakuḍ** (broom) or **golonakuḍ** (rake)—may or may not be possessed. Nouns formed by adding only the **-a** suffix always appear in a possessive construction: **ñ-wosona** (the thing that I swept); **ñ-golona** (the thing that I raked).

The large majority of Papago verbs act like **woson** when they are turned into nouns. We can state this simply: to change a verb into a noun, first add to the **imperfective** form of the verb the suffix **-a.** The following is another example:

golon	raking	a. **ñ-golon*a***	the thing that I raked; my raking
		b. **golon*a*kuḍ**	instrument for raking, rake

In the examples above with the **-a** suffix, **-a** is attached to an imperfectiv form which *ends in a consonant.* If the imperfective form of a verb *ends in a vowel,* the suffix **-a** does not appear:

cicwi	playing	a. **t-cicwi**	our game, competition
		b. **cicwikuḍ**	instrument used to play with; toy

NOTE: The plurals of these nouns are formed from the imperfective plural verb forms: e.g., **ñ-wakona** (the thing that I washed), **ñ-wapkona** (the things that I washed); **pa:ntakuḍ** (oven), **papantakuḍ** (ovens).

NOTE: One noun formed from a verb (**ñ-o'ohana**) has been used so frequently that it has become a regular noun in its own right. As such, it no longer requires the possessive construction and is simply **'o'ohana** (book).

THE MODIFIED IMPERFECTIVE IN POSSESSIVE CONSTRUCTIONS

The special form can be a noun if it occurs in a possessive construction; all of the (a) examples above illustrate this possibility. Consider also the following list, which illustrates certain characteristics about the nouns formed from the modified imperfective forms of transitive and intransitive verbs and from verbs that implicitly involve an object:

Verb	*Noun*
ce'ewid covering	**Klisti:na ce'ewida** the thing that Christina covered; Christina's covering
ceposid branding	**ñ-ceposida** my branding, the thing that I branded
cipkan working	**ñ-cipkana** my work, my position
gatwid shooting	**ha-gatwida** that thing that they shot
kuint counting	**ñ-kuinta** the things that I counted
na:d making a fire	**ñ-na:da** my fire, the fire that I made
nolawt buying	**t-nolawta** the thing that we bought
pa:nt making bread	**ñ-pa:nta** the bread that I baked
pikcult taking, making a picture	**ñ-pikculta** the picture I took or made
si:ṣp pinning	**ñ-si:ṣpa** the thing that I pinned
ṣonwuin hitting, pounding	**ñ-ṣonwuina** the thing that I pounded; my pounding
ta:tṣ parting	**ñ-ta:tṣa** the part that I made (*in hair*)
wakon washing	**m-wakona** your washing; the thing that I washed
wu:ḍ tying	**ñ-wuḍa** the thing that I tied up

NOTE: In general, a noun formed in this fashion from a simple *transitive* verb identifies the thing which is acted upon by the verb —for example, **ñ-kuinta** (the things that I counted). Nouns formed from verbs which implicitly involve an object—as, for example, **pikcult, pa:nt, na:d**—are similar. A noun formed from a simple *intransitive* verb identifies the action of the verb, for example **ñ-cipkana** (my work). And nouns formed from verbs which are either transitive or intransitive, as **'o'ohan** or **wakon,** can mean either.

The following is a list of verbs which *cannot* be made into this type of noun.

ba'a	swallowing	**'i'ihog**	coughing
bisc	sneezing	**je:k**	tasting
cendad	kissing	**ju:k**	raining
he'eḍkad	smiling	**ka:**	hearing
hehem	laughing	**ke:k**	standing
hewek	smelling	**meḍ**	running
him	walking	**ñeok**	speaking
hi:nk	barking; yelling	**si'i**	sucking
'i:bhe	breathing	**toḍk**	snoring

That is, none of these verbs can appear in a possessive construction in order to form a noun. We cannot say, for example, ***ñ-heweka** or ***ñ-ba'a.** It is interesting to note that, except for **ju:k,** all of these verbs have to do with normal activities of various parts of the body.

The following sentences illustrate the use of nouns formed by possessive construction:

1. **Hegai cu:hug 'o ḍ ñ-ṣonwuina.** That meat is/was the thing that I pounded.
2. **Hegai wisilo 'o ḍ Husi ceposida.** That calf is/was the thing that Joe branded (*literal:* Joe's branding).
3. **Hegai 'o ḍ ñ-nolawta.** That is/was the thing that I bought.
4. **Hewel 'at jeweḍmad g ñ-wapkona.** The wind got my wash dirty. (*Literal:* The wind put dirt on the things that I washed.)
5. **Nap ñeid g ñ-pikculta.** Do/did you see my photograph? (*Literal:* Are you seeing the picture that I made?)
6. **Mali:ya 'o taicu g ñ-pa:nta.** Mary wants (is/was wanting) the bread that I made.

7. **Ḍ ’o ’aṣ ’a’al ha-cicwi.** It is/was just a children’s game.
8. **Ḍ ’o Husi kuinta hegai lial.** That money is/was what Joe counted.

EXERCISES USING POSSESSIVE CONSTRUCTION

A. Turn the following modified verb forms into nouns (by using them in a possessive construction) in a sentence.

1. pisalta
2. kuinta
3. wuḍa
4. na:da
5. pa:nta
6. ta:tṣa
7. pikculta
8. nolawta
9. ceposida
10. cipkana

B. For native speakers only. Change the following imperfective verbs into nouns, give a definition for the noun, and use this noun in a sentence.

1. hihidoḍ
2. ṣa:mud
3. huhu’id
4. ñu:kud
5. kuḍut
6. hukṣan
7. hikck
8. ’eñigadad

THE MODIFIED IMPERFECTIVE PLUS THE SUFFIX -KUḌ

The modified form of the verb discussed above can also become a noun if it takes the suffix **-kuḍ**; all of the (b) examples in the first part of this lesson illustrate this possibility. More are given below:

Imperfective Singular Plus -a	*Noun Form With -kuḍ*	
ce'ewida	**ce'ewidakuḍ**	instrument used to cover with; blanket
gatwida	**gatwidakuḍ**	instrument used to shoot with; gun
kuinta	**kuintakuḍ**	instrument used to count with; possibly a calculator or ruler
na:da	**na:dakuḍ**	instrument used for making a fire; a stove
nolawta	**nolawtakuḍ**	instrument used to buy with; money; instrument used to buy at; store
pa:nta	**pa:ntakuḍ**	instrument used to make bread; oven
pikculta	**pikcultakuḍ**	instrument used to take a picture with; camera
pisalta	**pisaltakuḍ**	instrument used to weigh with; scale
si:ṣpa	**si:ṣpakuḍ**	instrument used to pin with; pin
ṣonwuina	**ṣonwuinakuḍ**	instrument used to pound with; rock, hammer
ta:tṣa	**ta:tṣakuḍ**	instrument used to make a part with; straight comb
wakona	**wakonakuḍ**	instrument used to wash with; basin, soap
wuḍa	**wuḍakuḍ**	instrument used to tie with; rope, twine

Remember that if the imperfective form of the verb ends in a vowel, the suffix **-a** will not appear; **-kuḍ** will, then, attach directly to the imperfective form, as in **cicwi, cicwikuḍ** or as in **gaswua, gaswuakuḍ** (instrument used to comb with; comb, brush).

The verbs **ce'ewid** and **ṣonwuin** have alternate imperfective forms—**ce'ewi** and **ṣonwui.** With both of these **-kuḍ** attaches directly.

ce'ewi	cover	**ce'ewikuḍ**	instrument used to cover, blanket
ṣonwui	pound	**ṣonwuikuḍ**	instrument used to pound with, rock, hammer

As the glosses of the nouns formed with **-kuḍ** suggest, this suffix makes a noun which means "the instrument used to do the action of the verb."

We discussed earlier in this chapter (see p. 99) a set of verbs which cannot be made into nouns by occurring in a possessive construction. In general, these same verbs do not normally take **-kuḍ.** Since these verbs refer, as we noted, to normal activities of various parts of the body, it is easy to see why they should not take **-kuḍ.** One does not need an instrument to smell or to taste or to feel.

It is important to note, however, that some of the verbs on that list do take **-kuḍ** quite normally. One example is **si'i:**

si'i	suck	**si'ikuḍ**	instrument used for sucking or to suck on, a nipple, a bottle

And others can, if some appropriate context is imagined. For example, although most people don't use an instrument to help them hear, there are such apparatuses and some people need them:

ka:	hear	**ka:kuḍ**	instrument to hear with, hearing aid

The following sentences illustrate the use of nouns formed with **-kuḍ:**

1. **'I:da 'o wuḍ ñ-wosonakuḍ.** This is my broom.
2. **No 'i:da ḍ m-si:ṣpakuḍ.** Is this your pin (safety pin)?
3. **Hegai 'o ḍ ñ-ce'ewidakuḍ.** That is my blanket.
4. **Golonakuḍ 'apt o hekaj k o golo g ṣa'i.** You will use the rake and rake the grass.
5. **Ḍ 'o ñ-pikcultakuḍ 'i:da.** This is my camera.

SPECIAL CASES: THE MODIFIED PERFECTIVE

The following verbs are irregular in that the special form of the verb which is the basis for making nouns is not the imperfective singular plus **-a.** Rather, in these cases the special form of the verb is based on the *perfective* singular. Note that a glottal stop occurs between the two vowels of the newly formed nouns.

Perfective Singular Verb		*Possessed Noun*		*Noun Formed with -kuḍ*	
woi	lay down	—		**wo'ikuḍ**	instrument used for lying down on, bed
gai	roasted	**ñ-ga'i**	the thing that I roasted	**ga'ikuḍ**	instrument used for roasting, grill
mua	killed	**ñ-mu'a**	the thing that I killed	**mu'akuḍ**	instrument used for killing (other than gun)

The verb **woson** (sweeping) can form a noun from the imperfective or the perfective form by adding **-kuḍ:**

wos	swept	**woskuḍ**	instrument used for sweeping, broom
woson	sweeping	**wosonakuḍ**	

EXERCISES USING THE SUFFIX **-KUḌ**

A. Translate the following sentences into Papago:

1. My comb is/was lying next to your shoes.
2. Joe's rake is/was (standing) behind the house.
3. Mary is/was cleaning the scale.
4. Where is your stove? (*Literal:* Where is your stove standing?)
5. Whose bottle (baby bottle) is this?
6. Is this your camera?
7. This is my washing machine.
8. Is this your gun?

B. Translate the following sentences into English:

1. No i:da wuḍ Husi golonakuḍ?
2. 'I:da 'o wuḍ Husi ta:tṣakuḍ.
3. 'A:pi 'apt 'an o wo'iwua wo'ikuḍ da:m k o koi.
4. Ga'ikuḍ da:m 'apt o gai g cu:kug.
5. No 'i:da ḍ m-pisaltakuḍ c m-kuintakuḍ?
6. Ñ-wapkonakuḍ 'o 'am ke:k ki: we:big.
7. Hegai 'o ḍ Mali:ya maḍ si'ikuḍ c cicwikuḍ.
8. No 'i:da ḍ m-ṣonwuikuḍ?

LESSON 16

Subordinate Clauses
The Clause Marker "m"

VOCABULARY

NOUNS

Singular		*Plural*	
huawĭ	deer	**huhuawĭ**	deer
ku'agĭ	wood	—	
'o'ohana	book	**o'ohana**	books
ṣa:yo	radio	**ṣaṣyo**	radios

VERBS

beihĭ *perf.*	got, purchased (*for someone*)	**u'i**	got, purchased (*for someone*)
bei *perf.*	got, purchased (*for oneself*)	**'ui**	got, purchased (*for oneself*)
ha'asa *perf.*	finished, completed	**ha'asa**	finished, completed
jiwa *perf.*	arrived	**dada**	arrived
jukto *perf.*	finished or stopped raining	—	
ka:c	lying (*an object*)	**we:c**	lying (*an object*)
mei *perf.*	burned (*inanimate object*)	**mei**	burned (*inanimate object*)
memḍa	running repeatedly	**wopo'o**	running repeatedly
mu: *perf.*	died	**koi**	died
mumku	being sick	**mumku**	being sick
s-ma:c	knowing, understanding	**s-ma:c**	knowing, understanding
s-wohocid	believing	**s-wohocid**	believing
wai *perf.*	called	**wai** *perf.*	called

ADJECTIVES

s-cuk	black	**s-cuck**	black
s-ke:gaj	pretty, good-looking, good	**s-ke:gaj**	pretty, good-looking, good
s-namkig	expensive	**s-nanamkig**	expensive

OTHER EXPRESSIONS

'am here
b 'o 'e-a:gĭ is/was said
b 'o 'e-elid he thinks
b 'o kaij g Huan John said
b 'o ñ-a:gid he told me
hekid when, after
ṣa if
'u:hum back (*where one came from*)
wenog while

MODIFYING CLAUSES USED AS ADJECTIVES

The following is an example of a modifying adjective clause:

1. **Hegai ceoj** ***mo cipkan*** **'o wuḍ ñ-we:nag.**
   MODIFYING CLAUSE

   That boy *that is working* is my brother.

The modifying clause **mo cipkan** describes something about the noun **ceoj** (boy); similarly, all adjective clauses modify the noun that directly precedes them. Consider the following examples:

2. **Hegai 'ali** ***mo ṣoak*** **'o wuḍ ñ-maḍ.**
   NOUN MODIFYING CLAUSE

   That child *that is crying* is my child.

3. **Hegai ki:** ***mo ge'ej*** **'o wuḍ Huan ki:.**
   NOUN MODIFYING CLAUSE

   That house *that is/was big* is/was John's house.

4. **Hegai 'o'ohana** ***mo 'an ka:c mi:sa da:m*** **'o s-cuk.**
NOUN MODIFYING CLAUSE
That book *that is/was (lying) on top of the table* is black.

Note that a noun with a modifying clause is regularly preceded by **hegai** or some other demonstrative. That is, say:

Hegai ceoj mo cipkan.

rather than:

***Ceoj mo cipkan.**

As these sentences illustrate, a modifying clause begins with the clause marker **m.** The auxiliary of the clause always attaches directly to the clause marker. The following chart lists the combinations of **m** and the auxiliary for both imperfective and perfective verb forms.

	Singular		*Plural*	
	IMPERFECTIVE	PERFECTIVE	IMPERFECTIVE	PERFECTIVE
1st per.	**mañ**	**mant**	**mac**	**matt**
2nd per.	**map**	**mapt**	**mam**	**mamt**
3rd per.	**mo**	**mat**	**mo**	**mat**

The following are more sentences with modifying clauses used as adjectives:

5. **Hegai 'oks mañ ñeid 'o wuḍ Huan je'e.** — That old lady that I saw (*literal:* I am/was seeing) is/was John's mother.
6. **Hegai ceoj mant we:m cipk 'o wuḍ Husi.** — That boy that I worked with is/was Joe.
7. **Hegai ma:gina map 'an da:m dahă 'o pi memḍa.** — That car that you are/were sitting on top of does/did not run.
8. **Nat mu: hegai huawĭ mapt gatwi?** — Did that deer you shot die?
9. **Hegai cu:hug mo am ka:c 'o s-namkig.** — That meat that is/was (lying) there is/was expensive.
10. **Hegai cehia mat 'am jiwa 'o wuḍ Mali:ya.** — That girl that arrived there is/was Maria.
11. **Hegam mac 'am ha-ñeid 'o wuḍ mamakai.** — Those (people) that are/were watching there are/were doctors.

12. **Hegai pa:l matt 'am wui ñeñeo 'o wuḍ ke:li.** That priest that we talked to is/was an old man.
13. **Nat jiwa hegai mant 'am wai?** Did that (person) that I called arrive (here)?
14. **No s-ke:gaj hegai ṣa:yo mapt bei?** Is/was that radio that you bought good?

MODIFYING CLAUSES USED AS ADVERBS

Adverbial clauses are also introduced by the clause marker **m.** The adverb itself is usually positioned inside the clause, after the aux. Notice also that often the adverb is optional [indicated by brackets].

15. **'Att o hihi 'u:hum mat [hekid] o jukto.** We will go back when it stops (will stop) raining.
16. **'Att o t-gegos mapt [hekid] o ha'icu hido.** We will eat when you cook (will cook) something.
17. **Mali:ya 'at ha-wapko g huhasaha'a mat [hekid] ha'asa ha'icu hihido.** Mary washed the dishes after she finished cooking something.
18. **Mat [hekid] 'am jiwa g Huan 'att t-gegos.** When John arrived we ate.
19. **Mat [hekid] mei g ku'agĭ 'att gai g cu:kug.** When the wood burned we roasted the meat.
20. **Mat o ṣa ju: att o hihi 'u:hum.** If it rains (will rain) we will go back.
21. **Att 'o t-gegos mapt o ṣa ha'icu hido.** We will eat if you cook (will cook) something.
22. **Mat ['am] o ṣa jiwa g Huan 'att o t-gegos.** If John arrives (will arrive) [here] we will eat.
23. **Mat o ṣa mei g ku'agĭ 'att o gai g cu:kug.** If the fire starts (will start) we will roast the meat.
24. **'A:ñi 'añ cipkan wenog mo mumku g Huan.** I am/was working while John is/was sick.

NOUN CLAUSES USED AS DIRECT OBJECTS

The following is an example of a noun clause used as a direct object:

25. **B 'o kaij hegai ceoj** ***mo cipkan g Huan.***
D. O. NOUN CLAUSE

That boy said *that John is working.*

A direct object noun clause shares with a modifying clause the property of beginning with the clause marker **m,** immediately followed by some form of the auxiliary. The difference is that a clause doesn't modify a noun, but rather acts like an object to the verb.

The following are more examples of noun clauses used as direct object:

26. **B 'o kaij g Husi mañ g ma:gina eñga.** Joe said that I own a car.
27. **B 'o 'e-elid g Husi mant g ma:gina bei.** Joe thinks that I bought a car.
28. **Hegai 'uwĭ 'o s-ma:c map 'a:pi mumku.** That woman knows (is knowing) that you are sick.
29. **B 'o ñ-a:gĭ hegai 'uwĭ mapt mumku ('a:pi).** That woman told me that you were sick.

EXERCISES

A. Translate the following sentences into English:

1. Hegai mi:stol mo s-cuk 'at 'i: g wi:b.
2. Hegai ke:li mo 'am dahă 'o ḍ makai.
3. B 'o kaij g Husi mo 'ab meḍ g Mali:ya.
4. B 'o 'e-elid g Mali:ya mo hegai 'am ki:.
5. Hegam cecia mo 'ab hihim 'o ḍ ñ-wepnag.
6. Hegam a'al mo 'am 'oyopo 'o pi ḍ ñ-wepnag.
7. Nap t-ñeid mac 'ab wo:po'ŏ?
8. Heu'u, 'em-ñeid 'ac mam 'ab wo:po'ŏ.

B. Using some of the simple sentences in the early lessons, write eight new sentences with subordinate clauses.

Stative Verbs, Adjectives, and Comparisons

VOCABULARY

NOUNS

Singular		*Plural*	
hemajkam	person	**hehemajkam**	persons, people
hidoḍ	cooked food, stew	**hihidoḍ**	cooked foods, stews
'ipuḍ	dress	**'i'ipuḍ**	dresses
kahon	box	**kakhon**	boxes
ko'okol	chile, spice	**ko'okol**	chiles, spices
lu:lsi	candy	**lu:lsi**	candies
taṣga	clock, watch	**taṣga**	clocks, watches

STATIVE VERBS AND ADJECTIVES

'ajij	(being) thin	**'a'ajij**	(being) thin
cemaj	(being) small	**ce'ecmaj**	(being) small
cewaj	(being) tall, long	**ce'ecwaj**	(being) tall, long
ge'ej, ge'e	(being) big	**ge'egḍaj, ge'egḍ**	(being) big
lo:go	(being) crazy	**lolgo**	(being) crazy
mumku	(being) sick	**mumku**	(being) sick
s-añi:lmagĭ	(being) blue	**s-ani:lmagĭ**	(being) blue
s-ap	(being) good, fine	**s-a'ap**	(being) good, fine
s-ba:bigĭ	(being) slow	**s-ba:bigĭ**	(being) slow
s-baga	(being) angry	**s-babga**	(being) angry
s-ce:dagĭ	(being) green	**s-cecdagĭ**	(being) green
s-cuk	(being) black	**s-cuck**	(being) black
s-da:pk	(being) slippery	**s-dadpk**	(being) slippery
s-gakĭ	(being) skinny	**s-gagkĭ**	(being) skinny
s-gi:g	(being) fat	**s-gi:gk**	(being) fat

STATIVE VERBS AND ADJECTIVES (*continued*)

Singular	*Plural*
s-he'ek (being) sour	**s-he'ek** (being) sour
s-he:pid (being) cold	**s-he:pid** (being) cold
s-hewhogĭ (being) cool	**s-hewhogĭ** (being) cool
s-hu:kĭ (being) warm	**s-hu:kĭ** (being) warm
s-i'owĭ (being) sweet, good-tasting	**s-i'owĭ** (being) sweet, good-tasting
siwĭ (being) bitter, sour	**siwĭ** (being) bitter
s-ju:k (being) deep	**s-ju:k** (being) deep
s-kaidag (being) loud	**s-kaidag** (being) loud
s-kawi:magĭ (being) brown	**s-kakawi:magĭ** (being) brown
s-kawk (being) hard	**s-kakawpk** (being) hard
s-ke:g (being) pretty, good-looking; good (*used to refer to a person*)	**s-ke:g** (being) pretty, good-looking; good
s-ke:gaj (being) pretty, good-looking, good (*used to refer to something other than a person*)	**s-ke:gaj** (being) pretty, good-looking, good
s-ko'ok (being) hot or spicy	**s-ko'ok** (being) hot or spicy
s-mohogĭ (being) itchy; scratchy	**s-momhogĭ** (being) itchy; scratchy
s-moik (being) soft	**s-momoik** (being) soft
s-mu'uk (being) sharp	**s-mu'umk** (being) sharp
s-nakosig (being) noisy	**s-nankosig** (being) noisy
s-nalaṣmagĭ (being) orange	**s-nanlaṣmagĭ** (being) orange
s-oam (being) yellow	**s-o'oam** (being) yellow
s-onk (being) salty	**s-o'onk** (being) salty
s-padma (being) lazy	**s-papdma** (being) lazy
s-tohă (being) white	**s-to:ta** (being) white
s-tonĭ (being) hot	**s-tonĭ** (being) hot
s-wagima (being) industrious	**s-wapagima** (being) industrious
s-we:c (being) heavy	**s-wepc** (being) heavy
s-wegĭ (being) red	**s-wepegĭ** (being) red
s-wihonig (being) messy	**s-wiphionig** (being) messy
ṣopolk (being) short	**ṣo'oṣpolk** (being) short
wecij (being) young	**wecij** (being) young

THE PREFIX **S-** ON STATIVE VERBS

The vast majority of vocabulary items in the list above can be used either as stative verbs or as adjectives. In this section, we are concerned with the first possibility.

Stative verbs are, in general, to be distinguished from other, nonstative, verbs in that they have the prefix **s-**. Not all stative verbs have the prefix **s-**; however, any verb with an **s-** prefix is a stative verb. The following sentences illustrate the vocabulary items used as stative verbs. They also indicate possible word orders.

1. a. **Husi kotoñ 'o s-tohă.**
   b. **S-tohă 'o g Husi kotoñ.** — Joe's shirt is/was white.
2. a. **Ñ-'o'ohanaga 'o s-cuk.**
   b. **S-cuk 'o g ñ-o'ohanaga.** — My book is/was black.
3. a. **Hegai 'ipuḍ 'o s-oam.**
   b. **S-oam 'o hegai 'ipuḍ.** — That dress is yellow.
4. a. **Huan gogsga 'o s-hemajima.**
   b. **S-hemajima 'o g Huan gogsga.** — John's dog is/was friendly.
5. a. **'A:cim 'ac ce'ecwaj.**
   b. **Ce'ecwaj 'ac 'a:cim.** — We are tall.
6. a. **Mali:ya maḍ 'o s-wagima.**
   b. **S-wagima 'o g Mali:ya maḍ.** — Maria's child is/was industrious.
7. a. **Ha-hidoḍ 'o s-tonĭ.**
   b. **S-tonĭ 'o g ha-hidoḍ.** — Their food is/was hot.
8. a. **S-he:pid 'o g ṣu:dagĭ.**
   b. **Ṣu:dagĭ 'o s-he:pid.** — The water is/was cold.
9. a. **S-hu:kĭ 'o g ñ-li:wa.**
   b. **Ñ-li:wa 'o s-hu:kĭ.** — My jacket is/was warm.

STATIVE VERBS IN NEGATIVE SENTENCES

Many of the stative verbs in the vocabulary list have an **s-** prefix. In the speech of many Papagos, the **s-** prefix is absent in negative sentences.

10. **Husi kotoñ 'o pi tohă.**
Joe shirt AUX NEG white.
Joe's shirt is/was not white.

Example (11) illustrates the dropped prefix and another position of the negative in sentences with a stative verb. In both (10) and (11) the negative directly precedes the stative verb.

11. **Pi tohă 'o g Husi kotoñ.**
NEG white AUX DET Joe shirt.
Joe's shirt is/was not white.

When the negative is initial to the sentence, the aux may come between the negative and the stative verb:

12. **Pi 'o tohă g Husi kotoñ.**
NEG AUX white DET Joe shirt.
Joe's shirt is/was not white.

Examples (10) through (12) illustrate all the possibilities for the position of the negative and the stative verb. That is, a sentence like (13), in which the negative does not precede the stative verb is not a good Papago sentence.

13. ***Tohă 'o pi g Husi kotoñ.**
white AUX NEG DET Joe shirt.

There is one exception to the rule about the relative position of the negative and the stative verb. If the stative verb is directly preceded by an adverb, the negative precedes the adverb.

14. a. **Mali:ya ko'okol hidoḍ 'o pi ṣa'i ko'ok.**
Mary chile stew AUX NEG ADVERB STATIVE VERB.

b. **Pi ṣa'i ko'ok g Mali:ya ko'okol hidoḍ.**
NEG ADVERB STATIVE VERB DET Mary chile stew.
Mary's chile stew is/was not really not.

In (14) the position of the negative is the same as in (10) and (11), except that the adverb **ṣa'i** intervenes between the negative and the stative verb. Note that (14b), unlike any other Papago sentence we have seen up to this point, lacks an aux. If there is an aux in such sentences, it follows *pi* and precedes the adverb, as shown in sentence (15):

15.	**Pi**	**'o**	**ṣa'i**	**ko'ok**	**g**	**Mali:ya**	**ko'okol**	**hidoḍ.**
	NEG	AUX	ADVERB	STATIVE VERB	DET	Mary	chile	stew

Mary's chile stew is/was not really hot.

But, a sentence like (16), in which the aux follows **ko'ok,** is not very good Papago. And a sentence like (17), in which the aux follows the adverb ṣa'i, or a sentence like (18), in which both the aux and the adverb ṣa'i follow the stative verb are not good at all.

16.	***Pi**	**ṣa'i**	**ko'ok**	**'o**	**g**	**Mali:ya**	**ko'okol**	**hidoḍ.**
	NEG	ADVERB	STATIVE VERB	AUX	DET	Mary	chile	stew

17.	***Pi**	**ṣa'i**	**'o**	**ko'ok**	**g**	**Mali:ya**	**ko'okol**	**hidoḍ.**
	NEG	ADVERB	AUX	STATIVE VERB	DET	Mary	chile	stew

18.	***Pi**	**ko'ok**	**'o**	**ṣa'i**	**g**	**Mali:ya**	**ko'okol**	**hidoḍ.**
	NEG	STATIVE VERB	AUX	ADVERB	DET	Mary	chile	stew

The following are more examples of negative sentences with stative verbs. Some have the s- prefix and some don't, to illustrate both possibilities for Papago speakers.

19. a. **'I:da lu:lsi 'o pi 'i'owĭ.**
    b. **Pi i'owĭ 'o 'i:da lu:lsi.**
    c. **Pi 'o 'i'owi 'i:da lu:lsi.**
    } This candy is/was not sweet.

20. a. **T-ma:maḍ 'o pi ṣa'i ṣoañ.**
    b. **Pi ṣa'i ṣoañ g t-ma:maḍ.**
    c. **Pi 'o ṣa'i ṣoañ g t-ma:mad.**
    } Our children are/were not really crying.

21. a. **'A:cim 'ac pi babga.**
    b. **Pi 'ac babga 'a:cim.**
    } We are not angry.

22. a. **Ha-ṣa:yo 'o pi ṣa'i kaidag.**
    b. **Pi ṣa'i kaidag g ha-ṣa:yo.**
    c. **Pi 'o ṣa'i kaidag g ha-ṣa:yo.**
    } Their radio is/was not really loud.

23. a. **Pi 'o ke:gaj g t-taṣga.**
    b. **T-taṣga 'o pi ke:gaj.**
    c. **Pi ke:gaj 'o g t-taṣga.**
    } Our watches are/were not good.

24. a. **Husi 'o:gĭ 'o pi ṣa'i si mumku.**
    b. **Pi ṣa'i si mumku g Husi 'o:gĭ.**
    c. **Pi 'o ṣa'i si mumku g Husi 'o:gĭ.**
    } Joe's father is/was not really very sick.

25\. a. **Hegai ko:ji mant mua ’o pi ṣa’i ge’ej.**
b. **Pi ṣa’i ge’ej hegai ko:ji mant mua.**
c. **Pi ’o ṣa’i ge’ej hegai ko:ji mant mua.**

That pig that I killed was not really big.

26\. a. **’I:da kahon mo s-wegĭ ’o pi ṣa’i we:c.**
b. **Pi ṣa’i we:c ’i:da kahon mo s-wegĭ.**
c. **Pi ’o ṣa’i we:c ’i:da kahon mo s-wegĭ.**

This box that is red is not really heavy.

ADJECTIVES

The vocabulary given at the beginning of the chapter can also be used as adjectives. These adjectives, taken from the imperfective singular and plural forms of the stative verb, can be used to modify singular or plural nouns in any type of sentence: transitive, intransitive, and copulative sentences with **wuḍ**. Some examples are shown below:

27\. **Hegam ge’egḍ s-kawi:magĭ ba:ban ’o ha-huhu’id hegam ce’ecem s-to:ta totobĭ.**

Those big brown coyotes are/were chasing the little white rabbits.

28\. **Hegai s-ke:g ’uwĭ ’o an ke:k ñ-we:nag hugidan.**

That attractive woman is/was standing next to my brother.

29\. **A:pi c Huan ’am s-a’ap wuḍ hehemajkam.**

You and John are/were good people.

Like other Papago sentences, these sentences with adjectives have a number of possible word orders, as shown in the following examples:

30\. a. **Klisti:na ’o s-ke:g wuḍ ’uwĭ.**
b. **S-ke:g ’o wuḍ ’uwĭ g Klisti:na.**
c. **Klisti:na ’o wuḍ s-ke:g ’uwi.**
d. **Ḍ ’o s-ke:g ’uwĭ g Klistina.**

Christina is/was an attractive woman.

31\. a. **Hegam s-papdma hehemajkam c a:pi ’am ’am s-ce:dagĭ kui weco daḍhă.**
b. **S-ce:dagĭ kui weco ’am daḍhă a:pi c hegam s-papdma hehemajkam.**
c. **A:pi c hegam s-papdma hehemajkam ’am ’am daḍhă s-ce:dagĭ kui weco.**

You (*sg.*) and those lazy people are/were sitting under a green tree.

32. a. **Mali:ya c 'a:ñi att bei g s-wegĭ 'ipuḍ c s-'añi:laṃagĭ kotoñ.**
    b. **'A:ñi c Mali:ya att bei g s-añi:lmagĭ kotoñ c s-wegĭ 'ipuḍ.**
    Mary and I bought the red dress and the blue shirt.

33. a. **Hegam s-wepegĭ ko'okol 'o wuḍ s-ko'ok ko'okol.**
    b. **Hegam s-wepegĭ ko'okol 'o s-ko'ok wuḍ ko'okol.**
    c. **S-ko'ok 'o wuḍ ko'okol hegam s-wepegĭ ko'okol.**
    d. **Ḍ 'o s-ko'ok ko'okol hegam s-wepegĭ ko'okol.**
    Those red chiles are/were hot chiles.

COMPARISONS IN PAPAGO

Comparisons between two things can be made by using stative verbs with the phrase **ba'ic 'i** (more) and the particle **ki** (than). The following sentences give some examples of this usage:

34. **Hegai ṣu:dagĭ 'o ba'ic 'i s-tonĭ ki 'i:da ṣu:dagĭ.**
    That water is/was hotter (*literal:* more hot) than this water.
35. **Ñ-we:nag 'o ba'ic i mumku ki 'a:ñi.**
    My brother/sister is/was sicker than I (am/was).
36. **Mali:ya gogogsga 'o ba'ic 'i s-hehemajima ki g Husi gogsga.**
    Maria's dogs are/were friendlier than Joe's dog.
37. **'I:da s-wegĭ ma:gina 'o ba'ic i s-nakosig ki hegai s-cuk ma:gina.**
    This red car is/was noisier than that black car.
38. **'Idam cecoj 'o ba'ic 'i ṣo'oṣpolk ki hegam 'u'uwĭ.**
    These boys are/were shorter than those women.
39. **'A:ñi 'añ ba'ic 'i ge'ej ki g ñ-we:nag.**
    I am/was bigger than my sister.

The superlative degree of comparison uses a stative verb with the phrase **ba'ic 'i** (more) and the particle **si** (very):

40. **Huan 'o ba'ic 'i si cewaj.** John is the tallest.
41. **Mali:ya 'o ba'ic 'i si s-ke:gaj.** Mary is the prettiest.

42. **Huan 'o ba'ic 'i si wecij.** John is the youngest.

43. **I:da hu:ñ 'o ba'ic 'i si s-i'owi.** This corn is the sweetest.

The only alternate word order for these comparative and superlative sentences is to have the phrase **ba'ic 'i** at the beginning of the sentence. For example:

44. **Ba'ic 'i 'o cewaj g Huan ki g Husi.** John is taller than Joe.

45. **Ba'ic 'i 'o si cewaj g Huan.** John is the tallest.

EXERCISES

A. Use each of the following words in two sentences. In the first sentence use these words as stative verbs and in the second use them as adjectives. Some of the sentences should be negative.

1. s-kawi:magĭ
2. s-añi:lmagĭ
3. s-nalaṣmagĭ
4. s-gi:g
5. s-gakĭ
6. lo:go
7. s-mohogĭ
8. s-baga
9. s-ju:k

B. *For native speakers only.* Use some stative verbs in perfective sentences. Explain what changes occur when the perfective form of the verb is used.

C. Give some sentences illustrating comparison in Papago. Use both comparative and superlative degrees.

LESSON 18

Numbers

VOCABULARY

NUMBERS

hemako one
go:k two
waik three
gi'ik four
hetasp five
cu:dp six
wewa'ak seven
gigi'ik eight
humuk nine
westma:m ten
gamai- *prefix added to one through nine for the teens*
gokko- twice, two times, the twenties
waikko- three times, thrice, the thirties
gi'ikko- four times, the forties
hetaspo- five times, the fifties
cu:dpo- six times, the sixties
wewa'akko- seven times, the seventies
gigi'ikko- eight times, the eighties
humukko- nine times, the nineties
siant- one hundred
mi:l- one thousand

NOUNS

Singular		*Plural*	
ha'a	pot, jar, bottle	**haha'a**	pots, jars, bottles
mansa:na	apple	**mansa:na**	apples
ṣaliwĭ	pair of pants	**ṣaṣliwĭ**	pairs of pants
'u'uhig	bird	**'u'uhig**	birds
wonam	hat	**wopnam**	hats

OTHER EXPRESSIONS

'eñga *v.*	owning	**'eñga**	owning
'eñga (*possessive pronoun or adj.*)	own	**'eñga**	own
he'ekio	how many	—	
taicu *v.*	wanting, desiring	**taicu**	wanting, desiring

COUNTING IN PAPAGO

To count from one to ten in Papago is fairly simple. The vocabulary list includes the numbers which are necessary.

one	**hemako**	three	**waik**
two	**go:k**	four	**gi'ik**

and so on up thru **westma:m** (ten).

To count from eleven to nineteen simply place the word **gamai** in front of the numbers one through nine. Thus the numbers would be as follows:

eleven	**gamai-hemako**	thirteen	**gamai-waik**
twelve	**gamai-go:k**	fourteen	**gamai-gi'ik**

and so on up to the number nineteen (**gamai-humuk**).

For the number twenty, the phrase would be **gokko-westma:n** (twice ten). Then, to count from twenty-one through twenty-nine, simply put **gokko** in front of the numbers one through nine as follows:

twenty-one	**gokko-hemako**	twenty-three	**gokko-waik**
twenty-two	**gokko-go:k**	twenty-four	**gokko-gi'ik**

and so on up to the number twenty-nine (**gokko-humuk**).

For the number thirty, the phrase is **waikko-westma:m** (three times ten), and the numbers from thirty-one through thirty-nine follow the same procedure as the twenties:

thirty-one	**waikko-hemako**	thirty-three	**waikko-waik**
thirty-two	**waikko-go:k**	thirty-four	**waikko-gi'ik**

and so on through the number thirty-nine (**waikko-humuk**).

The number forty is **gi'ikko-westma:m** (four times ten), and the forties begin in the same procedure as the other numbers.

forty-one	**gi'ikko-hemako**
forty-two	**gi'ikko-go:k**

and so on, again up to forty-nine (**gi'ikko-humuk**).

This same procedure continues with all the numbers up to ninety-nine (**humukko-humuk**), after which the number is one hundred (**siant**). Then the procedure begins again, so for the number one hundred one it would be **hemako-siant hemako** or for:

one hundred ten	**hemako-siant westma:m**
one hundred fifteen	**hemako-siant gamai-hetasp**
one hundred thirty	**hemako-siant waikko-westma:m**
two hundred five	**go:k-siant hetasp**
five hundred twenty-five	**hetasp-siant gokko-hetasp**
nine hundred ninety-nine	**humuk-siant humukko-humuk**

NUMBERS IN SENTENCES

1. **Hegam waik 'u'uwĭ mo gaḍhu 'oyopo 'o wuḍ ñ-wepnag.**
   Those three women that are walking around over there are my sisters.
2. **Hegam go:k mimstol c hegam hetasp gogogs 'o wuḍ Mali:ya 'eñiga.**
   Those two cats and those five dogs are Mary's (own).
3. **Hemako gogs 'at t-huhu'i.**
   One dog chased us.
4. **Westma:m mansa:na 'o ha-taicu g Husi k g Mali:ya gokko-westma:m ha-taicu.**
   Joe wants ten apples and Mary wants twenty apples.

5. **Gamai-hetasp 'att ha-nolawt g haha'a.**
   We bought fifteen pots.
6. **Waikko-waik hemajkam 'o 'am 'e-gegosid.**
   Thirty-three people are eating there.
7. **Pa:ncu 'o cu:dp ṣaṣliwĭ ha-wapkon.**
   Frank is washing six (pairs of) pants.
8. **Wewa'ak ba:ban 'o ganhu wo:po'o.**
   Seven coyotes are running way over there.
9. **Hemako siant 'o'ohana 'añ ha-taicu 'a:ñi.**
   I want one hundred books.
10. **Huan 'o hetaspo-waik ha-eñga g totobĭ k g Husi cu:dpo-humuk ha-eñga g cu:wĭ.**
    John owns fifty-three cottontails and Joe owns sixty-nine jackrabbits.

HOW MANY QUESTIONS

In Lesson 9 we discussed *who* (*whom*), *what*, and *where* questions. To ask *how many* questions is similar. The question word, **he'ekio,** can occur in pre-aux or post-aux position:

11. a. ***He'ekio*** **'apt o ha-nolawt g cucul 'a:pi?**
    PRE-AUX POSITION
    b. **'Apt** ***he'ekio*** **o ha-nolawt g cucul 'a:pi?**
    POST-AUX POSITION

    } How many chickens will you (are you going to) buy?

Consider, now, the following sentence:

c. **'Apt 'a:pi** ***he'ekio*** **o ha-nolawt g cucul?**

In (11c) **he'ekio** is in neither pre-aux nor post-aux position; rather, it follows **'a:pi.** The following example, which is not a good Papago sentence, suggests a restriction on the position of **he'ekio**—that is, **he'ekio** cannot occur after the verb:

d. ***'Apt o ha-nolawt** ***he'ekio*** **g cucul 'a:pi?**

One other important thing to note about *how many* questions is that the special form of the aux used in *who, what,* or *where* questions in the third person imperfective and perfective (**K** and **T,** respectively) is also used in *how many* questions when the aux is initial to the sentence.

12. a. **He'ekio 'o ha-eñga g gogogs g Husi?**
    b. **K he'ekio ha-eñga g gogogs g Husi?**
    c. **K g Husi he'ekio ha-eñga g gogogs?**
    How many dogs does Joe own?

The following are more examples of *how many* questions:

13. a. **T he'ekio ha-nolawt g Husi g papan?**
    b. **T g Husi he'ekio ha-nolawt g papan?**
    c. **He'ekio 'at ha-nolawt g papan g Husi?**
    How many loaves of bread did Joe buy?

14. a. **He'ekio 'o ha-eñga g 'i'ipud g Mali:ya?**
    b. **K g Mali:ya he'ekio ha-eñga 'i'ipud?**
    c. **K he'ekio ha-eñga g 'i'ipud g Mali:ya?**
    How many dresses does Mary own?

15. a. **He'ekio 'at ha-gagtwi g 'u'uhig g Pa:ncu?**
    b. **T he'ekio ha-gagtwi g 'u'uhig g Pa:ncu?**
    c. **T g Pa:ncu he'ekio ha-gagtwi g 'u'uhig?**
    How many birds did Frank shoot?

16. a. **He'ekio 'o ha-'eñga g Klisti:na g gagswuakuḍ?**
    b. **K g Klisti:na he'ekio ha-eñga g gagswuakuḍ?**
    c. **K he'ekio ha-'eñga g Klisti:na g gagswuakuḍ?**
    How many combs does Christina own?

17. a. **T he'ekio ṣaṣliwĭ c koktoñ ha-wapko g Mali:ya?**
    b. **T g Mali:ya he'ekio ṣaṣliwĭ c koktoñ ha-wapko?**
    c. **He'ekio 'at ha-wapko g Mali:ya g ṣaṣliwĭ c koktoñ?**
    How many pants and shirts did Mary wash?

18. a. **T he'ekio cu:wĭ o ha-hihido g m-hu'ul?**
    b. **T g cu:wĭ he'ekio o ha-hihido g m-hu'ul?**
    c. **He'ekio cu:wĭ 'at o ha-hihido g m-hu'ul?**
    How many rabbits is your grandmother going to cook?

19. a. **T he'ekio wopnam ha-nolawt g Husi 'am Cuk Ṣon 'am?**
    b. **T g Husi he'ekio wopnam ha-nolawt 'am Cuk Ṣon 'am?**
    c. **He'ekio 'at ha-nolawt g wopnam g Husi 'am Cuk Ṣon 'am?**
    How many hats did Joe buy in Tucson?

EXERCISES

A. Make up five Papago sentences that use numbers.

B. Make up some questions in Papago using the phrase *how many,* and answer them using the numbers, again in Papago.

Imperatives

VOCABULARY

NOUNS

Singular	*Plural*
bo:l ball	**bobol** balls
lial money	—
'u:s stick, board	**'u'us** sticks, boards

VERBS

ba:ñimad crawling	**ba:bañimad** crawling
cei *perf.* said	**cei** said
da'a jumping, flying	**ñe:ñe'e** jumping, flying
gei *perf.* fell	**ṣul** fell
hu: *perf.* ate	**hu:** ate
huḍ *perf.* came down	**huhuḍ** came down
ju: *perf.* did	**ju:** did
ma: *perf.* gave	**ma:** gave
ma'ihi *perf.* hit (*someone or something*) with an object	**ma'ihi** hit (*someone or something*) with an object
mel *perf.* arrived	**wo'i** arrived
ta:t *perf.* touched	**ta:t** touched
'ul *perf.* stuck out	**'u'ul** stuck out
wamigĭ, wamigid getting up	**wa:pamigĭ, wa:pamigid** getting up
wo'iwa *perf.* lay down	**wo:po'iwa** lay down
wu:ṣ *perf.* got out, came out	**wuha** got out, came out
wu:ṣad taking out	**wu:ṣad** taking out

OTHER EXPRESSIONS

'oig go ahead (*used to give permission*)

SIMPLE IMPERATIVE

There are different ways of forming imperatives in Papago. The most common is to attach the suffix **-iñ** to the imperfective verb (singular or plural form):

Imperfective		*Imperative*	
cipkan	working	**cipkaniñ**	work!
ñeok	talking	**ñeokiñ**	talk!
ñeñok	talking (*pl.*)	**ñeñokiñ**	talk! (*pl.*)
hihim	going, walking (*pl.*)	**hihimiñ**	go! walk! (*pl.*)

If the imperfective verb ends in a vowel, only the suffix **-ñ** is attached:

cicwi	playing	**cicwiñ**	play!
e-wacwi	swimming, bathing	**e-wacwiñ**	swim! bathe!

NOTE: If the verb is intransitive, the imperative form agrees in number with the subject. For transitive verbs, the object of the imperative form is understood from the context. In Lesson 6 we observed that a transitive verb agrees in number with its direct object. The same is true for the object of the imperative form of the verb. Therefore, if a plural object is implied, the imperative form of the verb must also be plural. Note also that the **ha-** prefix is used if the third person plural direct object is expressed. If the direct object is only implied, the **ha-** prefix is dropped.

Example

wakoniñ wash it! **wapkoniñ** wash them!

The following are examples of these imperatives:

1. **Cecposidiñ!** Brand them!
2. **Ṣa:mudiñ!** Herd (or shoo) it!
3. **Gaswuañ!** Comb your hair!
4. **Hihimiñ!** Walk! *or* Go! (*pl.*)
5. **Gagtwidiñ!** Shoot them!
6. **Gegosidiñ!** Feed it!
7. **Huhu'idiñ!** Chase it!
8. **Hihidodiñ!** Cook! Start cooking!

The other two ways to form the simple imperative in Papago are like the first in that they require the suffix **-iñ** or **-ñ.** But with some verbs this suffix must be attached to the perfective form of the verb:

Perfective		*Imperative*	
keickwa	kicked	**keickwañ**	kick it! *or*, kick it away!
kekiwa	stood	**kekiwañ**	stand up!
ṣonhi	hit	**ṣonhiñ**	hit it!

Finally, some verbs have irregular imperative forms. Examples are:

Imperative	
ba'iñ	swallow (it)!
behiñ	take (it)!
ce'iñ	say (it)!
dahiñ	sit!
hugiñ	eat (it)!
'i'iñ	drink (it)!
ma:kiñ	give (it)!
meliñ	run!
ñe'iñ	sing!
wo:po'iñ	run! (*pl.*)

NOTE: The retroflex consonants **ṣ** and **ḍ** can never have the vowel **i** following them. So when the suffix **-iñ** is attached either the **i** becomes **a**—for example, **wuṣ** becomes **wu:ṣañ** (get out!)—or the retroflex consonant becomes a regular **s** or **d**—for example **ko:ṣ** becomes **ko:siñ** (go to sleep!) and **huḍ** becomes **hudiñ** (come down!).

The following are imperative sentences:

1. **Hihimiñ 'am ha-ki: wui!** Go (*pl.*) to their house!
2. **Husi, meliñ 'am tianda wui!** Joe, run to the store!
3. **Si keickwañ g bo:l!** Really kick the ball!
4. **Behiñ g lial!** Take the money!
5. **Hugiñ g mu:ñ!** Eat the beans!
6. **'I'iñ g ṣu:dagĭ!** Drink the water!
7. **Gegosidiñ g 'ali!** Feed the child!
8. **Ṣa:mudiñ g gogs!** Shoo the dog away!
9. **'Oig ñe'iñ!** Go ahead and sing!
10. **Ha-cecposidiñ g wipsilo!** Brand the calves!

DIRECTIONAL IMPERATIVES

Another type of imperative is the *directional imperative.* All directional imperatives take the prefix **'i-**. In most cases, this prefix is attached to the imperfective verb form.

Imperfective		*Directional Imperative*	
ba:ñimad	crawling	**'i-ba:ñimad**	crawl this way!
gaswua	combing	**'i-gaswua**	comb (it)!
hihim	coming (*pl.*)	**'i-hihim**	come here! (*pl.*)
huhu'id	chasing	**'i-huhu'id**	chase (it) this way!
ṣa:mud	herding, shooing	**'i-ṣa:mud**	herd (it) this way, shoo (it) this way!
wamigĭ	getting up	**'i-wamigid**	get (it) up!
wapkon	washing (*pl.*)	**'i-wapkon**	wash them! (*pl.*)

However, with some verbs, the prefix is attached to the perfective form; in these cases, the verb also takes the suffix **-iñ** or **-ñ.**

Perfective		*Directional Imperative*	
huḍ	came down	**'i-huḍiñ**	come down!
'ul	stuck out	**'i-uliñ**	stick (it) out this way!
wu:ṣ	came out	**'i-wu:ṣañ**	come outside!

The verbs **gaswua** and **ṣa:mud,** which were given in the first list above as examples of the most common type of directional imperative, also have a directional imperative form like that in the second list: **'i-gaswuañ** (comb it!) and **'i-ṣa:mudiñ** (shoo it this way!). Since the perfective forms of **gaswua** and **ṣa:mud** are the same as the imperfective, these alternative forms are regular cases of the directional imperative formed from perfective verbs.

As with the simple imperative, a few verbs are totally irregular, in that the prefix **'i-** attaches to a special form.

	Imperative
'i-be:'i	bring (it) over here!
'i-da:'i	jump down!
'i-hi:m	come here!
'i-me:l	run over here!

In most of the directional imperatives, the speaker is requesting some movement. Thus, not all verbs can take the prefix **'i-**; in general, only verbs which indicate movement can take this prefix. The following verbs, for example, are not possible with **'i-**: **ceposid** (branding), **ñeok** (talking), or **hihidod** (cooking).

In fact, in most cases of the directional imperative the speaker is not only requesting some movement, but is also requesting some movement toward the speaker. For example, **'i-hi:m** (come here!) means (come here [toward the speaker]!) and **'i-me:l** (run over here!) means (run over here [toward the speaker]!). However, for some directional imperatives the movement involved is not specifically toward the speaker, but rather is just some forward or positive movement. Consider, for example,

'i-hudiñ come down! *or* get down!

'i-wu:ṣañ come out! *or* get out!

In either of these cases, the position of the speaker may or may not be the same as the hearer. If the speaker and the hearer were inside a house, for example, the speaker could tell the hearer to go outside by using **'i-wu:sañ,** but if the speaker were outside the house, the same directional imperative could be used and would mean "come outside!".

NOTE: The direction of movement can be directly specified by using specifiers or locatives (see Lesson 8) with the directional imperative form. Note that the specifier is followed by **g.** For example:

'ab **g 'i-wu:ṣañ** come outside (toward the speaker)!

'am **g 'i-wu:ṣañ** go outside (away from the speaker)!

At this point, however, we will not worry about specifying the direction of movement for such imperatives.

The following are examples of sentences with the directional imperative:

11. **'I-be:'i! 'Ant o ñei.** Bring (it) here! I will see (it).
12. **'I-hi:m! 'Ant o ha'icu m-ma:.** Come over here! I will give you something.
13. **'I-be:'i hegai kahon! 'Ant o ñei ṣa:cu 'o 'am 'eḍa wo'o.** Bring that box over here! I will see what is lying in (it).
14. **'I-wamigid g 'ali!** Get the baby up!
15. **'I-uliñ g nowij! 'Ant o ñei mat hebai 'e-hikc.** Stick his hand out this way! I will see where he cut himself.
16. **Mali:ya! 'I-me:l! 'Att o ha'icu hihido.** Mary! Run over here! We will cook something.
17. **B 'o kaij g ñ-je'e, "I-gaswua g mo'oj!"** My mother said, "Comb her hair!"

18. **'I-wu:ṣañ 'am jekkad! 'Ant o ha'icu m-ma:.**	Come outside! I will give you something.
19. **'I-be:'i hegai 'u:s! 'Ant o nai.**	Bring that stick! I will make a fire.
20. **'I-hudiñ! 'Ant o ha'icu m-a:gĭ.**	Get down! I'll tell you something.

EXERCISES

A. Give ten sentences in Papago using both types of imperatives.

B. Translate into English:

1. Meliñ 'am Husi ki: wui!
2. 'Oig ko:siñ! Pi 'apt o wam si'alim.
3. Sa:mudiñ g mumuwal! 'Am 'at o gei ñ-mu:ñ 'eḍa.
4. Dahiñ! 'Att o cicwi.
5. 'I-gaswuañ g 'ali mo'o! S-wihonig 'o.
6. Behiñ 'i:da! Ḍ 'o m-'eñga.
7. Wakoniñ g Husi mo'o! S-bi:dagĭ 'o.
8. Huhu'idiñ g gogs! 'At o hu: g ñ-hidoḍ.

C. *For native speakers only*. Translate the following sentences into English:

1. 'Oig, tt o hihi.
2. Him k dahiwañ.
3. Dahiñ k 'e-gegosid.
4. 'Oig hi:m tt o wo:p.
5. Meliñ k 'am ha-a:gid.
6. 'Ab g 'i-wu:ṣañ 'ant o m-ñei.
7. 'Am g 'i-wu:ṣañ 'atṣ o m-ñei.
8. 'I-'at gei! 'I-wamigid!
9. 'I-ñ-ma:k hegai, nt o hekaj.
10. 'I-uliñ ñ-wui nt o ñei.

LESSON 20

Word Order

VOCABULARY

NOUNS

Singular		*Plural*	
daikuḍ	chair	**dadaikuḍ**	chairs
'e'eñga	item of clothing	**'e'eñga**	clothes
ṣa'i	grass, hay	**ṣa'i**	grasses, hay
tlo:gi	truck	**tlolgi**	trucks

SIMPLE INTRANSITIVE AND TRANSITIVE SENTENCES

At various points in these lessons we have discussed word order ossibilities. In Lesson 1 we mentioned the fact that subject and verb in simple intransitive sentences can occur either in the order *subject-verb* or the order *verb-subject.*

1. a. **Hegai ceoj 'o ko:ṣ.**
   SUBJECT AUX VERB
   b. **Ko:ṣ 'o hegai ceoj.**
   VERB AUX SUBJECT
   } That boy is/was sleeping.

2. a. **Hegam 'a'al 'o ṣoañ.**
   SUBJECT AUX VERB
   b. **Ṣoañ 'o hegam 'a'al.**
   VERB AUX SUBJECT
   } Those children are/were crying.

We also discussed the word order possibilities in transitive sentences.

3.

a.	**Huan**	**'o**	**wakon**	**g ma:gina.**
	SUBJECT	AUX	VERB	OBJECT
b.	**Huan**	**'o**	**g ma:gina**	**wakon.**
	SUBJECT	AUX	OBJECT	VERB
c.	**Wakon**	**'o**	**g ma:gina**	**g Huan.**
	VERB	AUX	OBJECT	SUBJECT
d.	**Wakon**	**'o**	**g Huan**	**g ma:gina.**
	VERB	AUX	SUBJECT	OBJECT
e.	**Ma:gina**	**'o**	**wakon**	**g Huan.**
	OBJECT	AUX	VERB	SUBJECT
f.	**Ma:gina**	**'o**	**g Huan**	**wakon.**
	OBJECT	AUX	SUBJECT	VERB

John is/was washing the car.

The above cases suggest that the only element in a sentence with a fixed position is the aux.

In this lesson we will review some important points about word order in Papago and introduce some new considerations. The types of sentences which will be discussed will be those with postpositional phrases, possessive constructions, modifying clauses, and the future element **o.**

POSTPOSITIONAL PHRASES

In Lesson 8 we discussed two word orders for postpositional phrases. Example (4) below illustrates them:

4.

a.	**Mali:ya**	**'o**	**'am**	**ki:**	**ba:ṣo**	**ke:k.**
			SPECIFIER	OBJECT	POSTPOSITION	
b.	**Mali:ya**	**'o**	**'am**	**ke:k**	**ki:**	**ba:ṣo.**
			SPECIFIER		OBJECT	POSTPOSITION

Mary is/was standing in front of the house.

In the (4a) sentence the elements of the postpositional phrase occur together in the order *specifier-object-postposition,* but in the (b) sentence the *object* and *postposition* are moved to the end of the sentence, leaving the *specifier* behind.

Consider the following two sentences:

c.	**Mali:ya**	**'o**	**'am**	**ba:ṣo**	**ke:k**	**g ki:.**
			SPECIFIER	POSTPOSITION		OBJECT

d. **Mali:ya 'o 'am ke:k ba:ṣo g ki:.**
SPECIFIER POSTPOSITION OBJECT

In (4c) only the *object* of the postposition has been moved to the end of the sentence. In (4d) both the *object* and the *postposition* have been moved to the end, but they occur in the reverse order from that found in (4b). Note also that when the *object* follows the *postposition* (examples 4c and 4d) the determiner **g** is present.

The following are examples of the four word-order possibilities for postpositional phrases discussed above.

5. a. **Huan 'o 'am do'ag we:big cipkan.**
   b. **Huan 'o 'am we:big cipkan g do'ag.**
   c. **Huan 'o 'am cipkan do'ag we:big.**
   d. **Huan 'o 'am cipkan we:big g do'ag.**

   John is/was working behind the mountain.

6. a. **Klisti:na 'o 'am kui weco dahă.**
   b. **Klisti:na 'o 'am weco dahă g kui.**
   c. **Klisti:na 'o 'am dahă kui weco.**
   d. **Klisti:na 'o 'am dahă weco g kui.**

   Christina is/was sitting under the tree.

7. a. **'U'uhig 'o 'an ṣu:dagĭ da:m da'a.**
   b. **'U'uhig 'o 'an da:m da'a g ṣu:dagĭ.**
   c. **'U'uhig 'o 'an da'a ṣu:dagĭ da:m.**
   d. **'U'uhig 'o 'an da'a da:m g ṣu:dagĭ.**

   The bird is/was flying over (above) the water.

8. a. **Husi 'alidag 'o 'am mi:sa hugidan cicwi.**
   b. **Husi 'alidag 'o 'am hugidan cicwi g mi:sa.**
   c. **Husi 'alidag 'o 'am cicwi mi:sa hugidan.**
   d. **Husi 'alidag 'o 'am cicwi hugidan g mi:sa.**

   Joe's child is/was playing next to the table.

POSSESSIVE CONSTRUCTIONS

In Lesson 12 we discussed word order in possessive constructions. The simplest possessive construction is like that illustrated in example (9):

9. **Husi tlo:gi 'o ge'ej.** Joe's truck is/was big.
   POSSESSOR POSSESSED

We also discussed the suffix **-ij** or **-j** as indicating a third person pronoun possessor:

10. **Tlo:gij 'o ge'ej.** His truck is/was big.

The simple possessive construction illustrated in (9) can have the order *possessed, possessor* as well, but, when it does, the possessed noun has the suffix **-ij** or **-j**.

11. **Tlo:gij** (POSSESSED) **g Husi** (POSSESSOR) **'o 'ge'ej.** Joe's truck is/was big.

Note also that the possessor takes the determiner **g** when it follows the possessed noun.

Consider now the following double possessive construction:

12. **Husi we:nag gogsga 'o ko:ṣ.** Joe's brother's dog is/was sleeping.

This possessive construction has a number of order possibilities.

13. a. **We:nagij g Husi gogsga 'o ko:ṣ.**
    b. **Ko:ṣ 'o gogsgaj g we:nagij g Husi.**
    } Joe's brother's dog is/was sleeping.

In (13a) **Husi,** the possessor of **we:nag,** follows it and **we:nag,** thus, has the **-ij** suffix and the **g** determiner.* **Gogsga** is not affected since its possessor, **we:nag,** still precedes it. In (13b) each possessed noun is followed by its possessor—**we:nag** follows **gogsga** and **Husi** follows **we:nag.** Thus, both possessed nouns take the suffix **-ij** or **-j** and the **g** determiner.

The following are more examples of possible word order in sentences with possessive constructions:

14. a. **Husi nowĭ 'ant ta:t.**
    b. **Nowij g Husi 'ant ta:t.**
    } I touched Joe's hand.

15. a. **Alwi:lto ṣoiga 'o s-hemajima.**
    b. **Ṣoigaj g Alwi:lto 'o s-hemajima.**
    } Albert's horse is/was friendly.

16. a. **Huan gogsga 'at gegos g Husi.**
    b. **Gogsgaj g Huan 'at gegos g Husi.**
    } Joe fed John's dog.

*The **g** determiner is dropped because **we:nag** is at the beginning of the sentence.

17. a. **Pa:ncu hu'ul 'at o kuint g lial.**
    b. **Hu'ulij g Pa:ncu 'at o kuint g lial.**
    } Frank's grandmother will count the money.

18. a. **Mali:ya maḍ cicwikuḍ 'o s-wegĭ.**
    b. **Maḍij g Mali:ya cicwikuḍ 'o s-wegĭ.**
    c. **Cicwikuḍaj g maḍij g Mali:ya 'o s-wegĭ.**
    } Mary's child's toy is/was red.

SUBORDINATE CLAUSES

In Lesson 16 we discussed subordinate clauses. The following is an example:

19. **Hegai ceoj *mat g Husi keihi* 'o ṣoak.**
    CLAUSE

    That boy *that Joe kicked* is/was crying.

In sentence (19) the clause, which begins with **mat**, can have another word order possibility:

20. **Hegai ceoj 'o ṣoak *mat g Husi keihi.***
    CLAUSE

    That boy *that Joe kicked* is/was crying.

We must also note that sentences with clauses like the one in (19) have the same word order possibilities discussed for intransitive and transitive sentences discussed in Lesson 1. For example, in (19) the entire subject—**hegai ceoj mat g Husi keihi**—and the verb—**ṣoak**—do not occur in a fixed position relative to one another.

21. **Ṣoak 'o hegai ceoj *mat g Husi keihi.***
    That boy *that Joe kicked* is/was crying.

The following sentences give more examples of word order in sentences with clauses:

22. a. **Hegai to:bĭ mat g Huan gatwi 'o ganhu meḍ.**
    b. **Hegai to:bĭ 'o ganhu meḍ mat g Huan gatwi.**
    c. **Ganhu 'o meḍ hegai to:bĭ mat g Huan gatwi.**
    That rabbit that John shot is/was running over there.

23. a. **Mat hekid o wam g 'ali 'att o wo:p 'am Cuk Ṣon wui.**
    b. **Att o wo:p 'am Cuk Ṣon wui mat hekid o wam g 'ali.**
    c. **Cuk Ṣon wui 'att o wo:p mat hekid o wam g 'ali.**
    When the baby gets up (wakes up), we will go to Tucson.

24. a. **Hegai ceoj mo g Huan we:m cipkan 'at pi jiwa.**
    b. **Hegai ceoj 'at pi jiwa mo g Huan we:m cipkan.**
    c. **Pi 'at jiwa hegai ceoj mo g Huan we:m cipkan.**
    That boy that John is/was working with did not arrive.

25. a. **B 'o ñ-a:gid g Mali:ya mapt 'a:pi g s-ke:g s-ce:dagĭ 'ipuḍ bei.**
    b. **Mali:ya 'o b ñ-a:gid mapt 'a:pi g s-ke:g s-ce:dagĭ 'ipuḍ bei.**
    c. **B 'o ñ-a:gid mapt g s-ke:g s-ce:dagĭ 'ipuḍ bei g Mali:ya.**
    Mary told me that you bought a pretty green dress.

26. a. **Hegai 'ali mo 'am ki: Cuk Ṣon 'am 'o ṣa'i si s-wagima.**
    b. **Hegai 'ali 'o ṣa'i si s-wagima mo 'am ki: Cuk Ṣon 'am.**
    c. **Ṣa'i si s-wagima hegai 'ali mo 'am ki: Cuk Ṣon 'am.**
    That child that is/was living in Tucson is/was really very industrious.

27. a. **Hegai ke:li mo 'am dahă ki: we:big 'o s-padma ḍ hemajkam.**
    b. **Hegai ke:li 'o s-padma ḍ hemajkam mo 'am dahă ki: we:big.**
    c. **S-padma 'o wuḍ hemajkam hegai ke:li mo 'am dahă ki: we:big.**
    That old man that is/was sitting behind the house is/was a lazy person.

28. a. **Hegai kawyu mat keihi g Husi 'o gaḍhu 'oimeḍ.**
    b. **Hegai kawyu 'o gaḍhu 'oimeḍ mat keihi g Husi.**
    c. **Gaḍhu 'o 'oimeḍ hegai kawyu mat keihi g Husi.**
    That horse that kicked Joe is/was walking way over there.

FUTURE CONSTRUCTIONS

In Lessons 10 and 11, two different forms of the future tense were introduced—the future perfective and the future imperfective, illustrated in examples (29) and (30), respectively.

29. **Ceoj 'at o ñeo.** The boy will speak.

30. **Ceoj 'at o ñeokad.** The boy will be speaking.

Sentences in either the future perfective or the future imperfective have a certain restriction on word order possibilities. First, the future marker **o** must precede the verb and the aux must directly precede the **o.** Thus, nothing can come between either **o** and the verb or between the aux and **o.** So, if the aux is second in the sentence, the only possible word order for an intransitive sentence is as shown in examples (29) and (30) and the only possible word orders for transitive sentences are those shown in examples (31) and (32).

31. a. **Mali:ya 'at o hihido g mu:ñ.**
    b. **Mu:ñ 'at o hihido g Mali:ya.**
    } Mary will cook the beans.

32. a. **Mali:ya 'at o hihidodad g mu:ñ.**
    b. **Mu:ñ 'at o hihidodad g Mali:ya.**
    } Mary will be cooking the beans.

There is another possible word order for sentences in the future:

33. **'At o ñeo g ceoj.** The boy will speak.

34. **'At o ñeokad g ceoj.** The boy will be speaking.

35. **'At o hihido g Mali:ya g mu:ñ.** Mary will cook the beans.

36. **'At o hihidodad g Mali:ya g mu:ñ.** Mary will be cooking the beans.

Note that sentences (33) through (36) are exceptions to the first rule of Papago grammar—the rule concerning the position of the aux. In these examples the aux occurs initial to the sentence. In future sentences it is possible for the aux to be initial, as long as it immediately precedes **o** and **o** immediately precedes the verb.

The following sentences give more examples of the future perfective and the future imperfective.

37. a. **Huan 'at o cipk.**
    b. **'At o cipk g Huan.**
    } John will work.

38. a. **Pa:ncu 'at o me: 'am tianda wui.**
    b. **'At o me: 'am tianda wui g Pa:ncu.**
    } Frank will run to the store.

39. a. **'A:cim 'att o wo:p 'am Husi ki: wui.**
    b. **'Att o wo:p 'am Husi ki: wui 'a:cim.**
    } We will go (are going to go) to Joe's house.

40. a. **'A:pim 'amt o ha-wapko g 'e'eñga.**
    b. **'Amt o ha-wapko g 'e'eñga 'a:pim.**
    c. **'E'eñga 'amt o ha-wapko 'a:pim.**
    } You (*pl.*) will wash the clothes.

41. a. **Husi 'at o ha-wapkonad g huhasaha'a.**
    b. **'At o ha-wapkonad g huhasaha'a g Husi.**
    c. **Huhasaha'a 'at o ha-wapkonad g Husi.**
    } Joe will be washing dishes.

42. a. **Klisti:na 'at o golonad g ṣa'i.**
    b. **'At o golonad g ṣa'i g Klisti:na.**
    c. **Ṣa'i 'at o golonad g Klisti:na.**

} Christina will be raking the grass.

43. a. **Hegai 'uwĭ 'at o gegosidad g 'ali.**
    b. **'At o gegosidad g 'ali hegai 'uwĭ.**
    c. **'Ali 'at o gegosidad hegai 'uwĭ.**

} That woman will be feeding the baby.

It should be pointed out that in sentences where the aux is in initial position, the first vowel is usually not pronounced. So **'at** is **t, 'apt** is **pt, 'amt** is **mt, 'att** is **tt,** and **'ant** is **nt;** but we will write the full form here.

EXERCISES

A. Translate the following sentences into Papago and give all the possible word orders for each one:

1. Mary's mother is coming.
2. Joe's cat was eating and drinking milk.
3. Frank is eating beside the river.
4. That girl that John hit is angry.
5. That man that I saw is coming.
6. That girl's hair is very black.
7. That child's mother's sister is sick.
8. Frank's sister's cooking is very good (good tasting).
9. That dog was sleeping under the chair.

B. Translate the following English sentences into Papago; give all the possible word orders:

1. It will be raining.
2. Mary will be cleaning tables in the morning (tomorrow).
3. John will be washing cars tomorrow.
4. We will be cooking the beef (*literal:* cow meat) tomorrow.
5. It will (is going to) rain.
6. Mary will clean the tables.
7. John will wash the cars.
8. We will cook the meat tomorrow.

Second Review Lesson

VERB FORMS

List the perfective, future perfective, and the future imperfective form for each of the following verbs, and then use each of the verbs —in any form except the imperfective—in a sentence.

1. ñeñok
2. ko:kṣ
3. cecposid
4. ñeid
5. wapkon
6. gegosid
7. gagswua
8. wua
9. 'oyopo
10. pa:nt
11. kuint
12. woson
13. pisalt
14. waid
15. s-ma:c

POSSESSION

Translate the following possessive constructions into Papago, and then use each phrase in a Papago sentence:

1. our heads
2. my feet
3. my saddle
4. their shovels
5. her basket
6. my mother's plate
7. our dogs
8. our horses
9. my brother's shirt
10. Joe's grandmother's trees
11. her land
12. the child's eye
13. your cattle
14. our houses
15. my mother's brother's chickens

WUḌ AND COMPARISONS

Translate the following sentences into English:

1. Hegai 'o wuḍ Huan ma:gina mo s-cuk c pi memda.
2. No 'a:pi wuḍ m-wepnag hegam 'u'uwĭ mat 'am dada m-ki: 'am?
3. No hegai ke:li mat 'am jiwa wuḍ Husi 'o:gĭ?
4. Hegai s-cuk gogs c hegai s-tohă gogs 'o wuḍ Pa:ncu eñga.
5. B 'o kaij g ñ-je'e mo hegai 'uwĭ ṣa'i si s-padma wuḍ hemajkam.
6. B 'o kaij g Mali:ya mo hegai 'ali mo mumku pi wuḍ ṣa'i ha-hajuñ.
7. Hegai s-cuk gogs 'o ba'ic 'i s-hemajima ki hegai s-tohă gogs.
8. Ḍ 'o Ju:kam hegai ke:li, pi 'o wuḍ ṣa'i Milga:n.
9. Ḍ 'añ ha-je'e?
10. Huan 'o ba'ic 'i cewaj ki g Husi.
11. Ḍ 'o hegam.
12. Mali:ya 'o ba'ic 'i s-ke:gac ki g Klisti:na.
13. No hegai Ju:kam ke:li wuḍ m-maistla?
14. B 'o kaij g Husi mo wuḍ makai hegai cehia mat 'ia mel tako.

MORPHOLOGY: NOUNS FROM VERBS AND VERBS FROM NOUNS

Give the appropriate word for each of the following:

1. soaping
2. peeling
3. instrument for raking, a rake
4. adding sugar to something
5. removing salt
6. applying medicine to, making well
7. instrument for sweeping, broom
8. removing by scratching
9. instrument for writing
10. powdering

11. instrument for weighing
12. flouring, adding flour to
13. spitting on something
14. instrument for taking pictures
15. removing by scraping
16. instrument used to pin with
17. removing fur
18. instrument to play with, toy
19. adding pepper to
20. instrument to pound with
21. instrument used to part hair with, comb
22. instrument to cover with
23. thing to lie on, bed
24. thing to sit on, chair
25. oiling, adding oil to

SUBORDINATE CLAUSES

Translate the following sentences:

1. Napt ha-nolawt hegai haiwañ mo gaḍhu kui weco wo'o?
2. Did you see those Oriental people that arrived here at their house?
3. Hegai 'uwĭ mat 'am jiwa 'o ḍ ñ-o:gĭ we:nag maḍ.
4. B 'o kaij g ṣa:yo mo 'ab him g ju:kĭ.
5. Those people think that it will rain tomorrow.
6. B 'o kaij g Husi mat 'ab wo:p hegam Mali:ya c Klisti:na.
7. Att o t-gegos mat (hekid) o jiwa g Huan.
8. Hegai 'ali mo 'am we:m cicwi g Klisti:na 'o wuḍ ñ-we:nag maḍ.
9. 'A:ñi 'añ s-ma:c hegai 'uwĭ mo 'am ke:k.
10. 'Ant o hi: 'u:hum mat o jukto.
11. B 'o 'e-elid g Husi mat g Huan 'am o me: hegai tianda wui mo ge'ej.

12. B 'o kaij g Huan matt 'a:cim 'am o wo:p k gaḍhu o ko:k Klistina je'e ki: 'am.
13. Is that John that is sitting there?
14. Hegai ceoj mat ñ-siswuimad 'o pi 'ap wuḍ hemajkam.
15. That woman that is making bread is my grandmother (maternal).

IMPERATIVES

Translate the following into English:

1. Meliñ 'am ha-ki: wui!
2. 'I-ñ-ma:k hegai!
3. 'I-hi:m! 'Ant o ha'icu m-ma:.
4. 'I-'uliñ! 'Ant o ñei.
5. Wo:po'iñ 'am Husi Ki:-wui k 'i-wamgid g 'u:s mat 'i-gei.
6. 'I-wu:ṣad g gogs.
7. Mali:ya, 'i-me:l!
8. 'I-be:'i hegai ga:t! 'Ant o ñei.
9. Ṣa:mudiñ g mi:stol!
10. Gegokiwañ! 'Att o hihi 'am ha-je'e wui.

PART III
Conversations in Papago

LESSON 21

Are You Going to the Dance?

VOCABULARY

NOUNS

Singular	*Plural*
'e-piast dance, feast (*Literal:* celebrating itself)	**'e-pipiast** dances, feasts

VERBS

ha'asa *perf.* quit, finished	**ha'asa** quit, finished
ju: *perf.* did	**wua** did
ma:c knowing	**ma: c** knowing
'oi *perf.* went with, followed	**'oi** went with, followed
s-wohom (being) true	**s-wohom** (being) true
'u'ad bringing	**'u'ad** bringing
waila dancing	**wapaila** dancing

OTHER EXPRESSIONS

ba 'e:p also
'ep another
hig what about, how about **'a:p hig** how about you? what about you? *The pronoun* **'a:p** *can be substituted by any other independent pronoun, usually in the short form* (**'a:ñ, heg, 'a:c, 'a:m,** etc.).
pegi 'oig okay
s-wohom really, truly
ta:pĭ don't know (*equivalent to shoulder shrug meaning "don't know"*)

DIALOG

Mali:ya	**Ba: tṣ 'ep o 'e-piast?** Where is there going to be another dance?
Huana	**Ta:pĭ, pi 'añ ma:c.** I don't know.
Mali:ya	**Napt 'am o hi:?** Are you going?
Huana	**Pi'a, ha'asa 'ant g waila. 'A:p hig?** No, I quit dancing. How about you?
Mali:ya	**'A:ñi ba 'e:p (ha'asa g waila).** Me too (quit dancing).
Huana	**S-wohom?** Really?
Mali:ya	**Si 'o s-wohom. Pi 'ant 'am o hi:.** It's really true. I'm not going.
Huana	**Ṣa: pt o 'e-ju:? Napt o 'oi g Eddi mat 'i o ṣa mel?** What are you going to do? Are you going with Eddie if he comes?
Mali:ya	**Mat o ṣa 'u'ad g lial, nt 'am o a hi:.** If he has money, I'll go.
Huana	**Pegi 'oig, nt o a 'ep m-ñei.** Okay, I'll see you later.

EXERCISES

A. Use each of the new nouns and verbs in an original sentence.

B. Illustrate the phrases **ba 'e:p** and **pi ma:c** in at least four original sentences.

Is This Word Papago?

VOCABULARY

NOUNS

Singular	*Plural*
ce:gig name	**cecgig** names
da:sa cup	**dadsa** cups
Jujkam ha-ñi'okĭ Spanish language	—
kuji:yo knife	**kuji:yo** knives
kusal spoon	**kuksal** spoons
tinidol fork	**tinidol** forks
'uskonakuḍ fork	**'u'uskonakuḍ** forks
wainom knife	**wapainom** knives
wa:so can	**wapso** cans

VERBS

'a'aga saying about, calling	**'a'aga** saying about, calling
behĕ getting, taking	**'u'u** getting, taking
kak'e asking	**kak'e** asking
s-ma:cim wanting to know	**s-mamcim** wanting to know

OTHER EXPRESSIONS

'ab 'amjeḍ about
na:'as wuḍ 'a'i hegai I guess that is all
ḍ 'a'i hegai that is all
'O'odhamkaj in Papago
ṣag wepo I guess, I think

DIALOG

Huan	**Ṣa: p a'i masma?** How are you?
Husi	**S-ape 'añ, a:p hig?** I'm well, and you?
Huan	**'A:ñi 'añ ba 'e:p m 'a'i s-ape. Taicu 'añ mant o ha'icu m-kak'e 'ab 'amjeḍ g 'O'odham ñi'okĭ.** I'm well also. I want to ask you something about the Papago language.
Husi	**Ha'u, m 'o a s-ape. B g ha'icu ñ-kak'e.** Yes, that's fine. Ask me something.
Huan	**Ṣa: m 'a'aga 'i:da 'O'odhamkaj?** What do you (*pl.*) call this in Papago?
Husi	**Heg 'ac hab 'a'aga *da:sa;* ha'i g 'O'odham 'o hab 'a'aga *wa:so.* Idam 'o 'ab Jujkam ha-ñi'okĭ 'amjeḍ behĕ g e-cecgig.** We call that a *cup;* some Papagos call it a *can.* The words are from the Spanish language.
Huan	**M 'i:da has 'a'aga?** And what do you (*pl.*) call this?
Husi	**Heg 'ac hab 'a'aga *huasa'a.*** We call that a *plate.*
Huan	**Ṣa:cu 'o wuḍ 'i:da?** And what is this?
Husi	**Heg 'o wuḍ *kusal.* 'Id 'o ba 'e:p 'ab Jujkam ha-ñi'okĭ 'amjeḍ behĕ g 'e-ce:gig.** That is a *spoon.* This word is also from the Spanish language.
Huan	**No 'i:da c 'i:da ba 'e:p 'ab Jujkam ha-ñi'okĭ 'amjeḍ behĕ g 'e-cecgig?** Do this thing and this thing also get their names from the Spanish language?
Husi	**Nt hig o ñei . . . 'I:da 'ac hab 'a'aga *'uskonakud.* Heg 'o am 'O'odham ñi'okĭ 'amjed, k 'aṣ hab 'a ha'i g 'O'odham hab 'a'aga *tinido:l.* 'Id 'o 'ab Jujkam ha-ñi'okĭ**

'amjeḍ. Hegai hema 'o wuḍ *wainom.* Ṣag wepo mo 'i:da pi 'abhu ṣa'i behĕ g 'e-ce:gig Jujkam ha-ñi'okĭ 'amjeḍ.
Let me see . . . This we call a *fork.* That is from the Papago language, but some Papagos call it *tinidol.* This is from the Spanish language. The other one is called a *knife.* I think that that is not from the Spanish language.

Huan **Nopi ha'i g 'o'odham ba 'e:p hab 'a'aga 'i:da *kuji:yo* mo ba 'e:p 'ab Jujkam ha-ñi'okĭ 'amjeḍ?**
Don't some people call this thing *kuji:yo,* which is also from the Spanish language?

Husi **'A: hau'u.**
Oh yes.

Huan **Pegi, na:'as wuḍ a'i hegai.**
Well, I guess that is all.

Husi **Pegi, nappi 'am 'i hekid o ṣa ha'icu s-ma:cimk 'i hahawa o ñ-ñei.**
Well, whenever you want to know something come and see me again.

Huan **Pegi 'oig, nt o a 'ep m-ñei.**
Okay, I'll see you again.

EXERCISES

A. Use each of the new nouns in an original Papago sentence.

B. Use each of the new verbs and expressions in an original Papago sentence.

C. Make four original Papago questions by following the question forms used in this dialogue.

LESSON 23

My Mother Is Sick

VOCABULARY

NOUNS

Singular	*Plural*
ṣomoigig cold	**ṣomoigig** cold

VERBS

'ai *perf.* caught, reached	**'ai** caught, reached
na:'as supposing, guessing	

OTHER EXPRESSIONS

ba but
b 'añ a ṣa ñ-'elid that is what I (kind of) think
k has cu'ig what's wrong . . .? what's the matter with . . .? *Any other form of the special form of the aux* (**p, m,** or **c**) *may be substituted for the* **k** *in this phrase.*
mañ 'aṣ 'i s-ape I am just fine (*Literal:* I am just good, all right)
pegi well

DIALOG

Klisti:na	**Ṣa: p a'i masma?** How are you?
Huana	**Mañ 'aṣ 'i s-ape. 'A:p hig?** I'm fine. How about you?
Klisti:na	**'A:ñi 'añ ba 'e:p m 'aṣ 'i s-ape.** I'm fine also.

Huana **Ṣa 'o 'a'i masma g m-je'e?**
How is your mother?

Klisti:na **Na:'as maṣ 'i s-ape. K 'a:pi g m-je'e has 'i masma?**
I assume she's fine. And how is your mother?

Huana **Pi 'o 'amhu'i si s-ape. Mumku 'o.**
She's not too well. She's sick.

Klisti:na **K has cu'ig?**
What's wrong?

Huana **Heg 'at 'ai ṣomoigig matp 'an 'oimed.**
She caught that cold that is apparently going around.

Klisti:na **'I: 'eda 'o pi ke:gaj mat heg hekaj o mumku hegam mo ḍ 'al 'o'okĭ c kekel.**
Oh no, it is not good for elderly people to be sick with that.

Huana **Ha'u, s-ma:c 'añ, ba g ñ-je'e hia s-ap 'e-ñu:kud.**
Yes, I know, but my mother takes good care of herself.

Klisti:na **Pegi, tphu'i hemu o wamik 'an 'ep o has memdad g m-je'e.**
Well, perhaps in a while your mother will be up and running around.

Huana **Ha'u, b 'añ a ṣa ñ-'elid.**
Yes, that is what I think.

EXERCISES

A. Use five of the new vocabulary words and phrases in some original sentences.

B. Use the phrase **k has cu'ig** in some original sentences. Substitute the **k** with any of the other special forms of the aux.

What Time Is It?

VOCABULARY

NOUNS

Singular	*Plural*
malioñ boss	**mamlioñ** bosses
malioñga my boss	**mamlioñga** my bosses
'o:la hour	**'o:la** hours

VERBS

'a: saying, calling names	**'a:** saying, calling names
'e-aihim reaching, coming upon (*Literal:* reaching itself)	**'e-aihim** reaching, coming upon
'e-bai'owc past (*Literal:* past itself	**'e-bai'owc** past
kak'e asking	**kak'e** asking
s-ma:ckad will be knowing	**s-ma:ckad** will be knowing
wi'is *perf.* left	**wi'is** left

OTHER EXPRESSIONS

ba but
'eḍa-hugkam half past (*the hour*)
-kĭ apparently (*suffix, attaches to the auxiliary*)
napi because he *To form the word "because" for the other persons and numbers, simply attach* **n + aux + pi.** *For example:* **n + ap + pi = nappi** (because you); **n + ac + pi = nacpi** (because we); *and so on.*
gamai-hemako-ceḍ at eleven *Note that the location marker* **-ceḍ** (*Literal:* in) *is used to mark the time of the hour. Thus,* **hemako-ceḍ** *translates as* "one o'clock."

He'ekio 'o 'a'i him g taṣ?
He'ekio 'o 'a'i him g 'o:la?
He'ekio 'o ḍ 'a'i?
} What time is it?

DIALOG

Huan **Ñ-nawoj, nap s-ma:c mo he'ekio ḍ a'i g 'o:la?**
My friend, do you know what time it is?

Husi **Pi 'añ ṣa'i ma:c. Na:'as 'e-aihim g gamai-hemako. Pi:wulo g kak'e. Heg 'at o s-ma:ckad napi ge taṣga.**
I don't know. It must be getting on toward eleven o'clock. Ask Pete. He'll know because he has a watch.

Huan **Pi:wulo, he'ekio 'o a'i him g taṣ?**
Pete, what time is it?

Piwulo **E-atkĭ 'ai g gamai-hemako 'eḍa-hugkam, ba 'a:ñi g ñ-taṣga 'aṣ si s-hottam him. Him k 'am kak'e g Mali:ya —heg 'at s-ap 'am o m-a:gĭ g 'o:la.**
Apparently it is eleven thirty, but my watch goes too fast. Go ask Mary—she will be able to tell you the right time.

Huan **Mali:ya, he'ekio 'o ḍ a'i g 'o:la?**
Mary, what time is it?

Mali:ya **Hetasp minu:do 'o 'am wi'is mat ḍ o gamai-hemako. 'A, b 'ant o cem cei hetasp minu:do 'at 'i 'e-ba'oiwc g gamai-hemako.**
It's five minutes to eleven. Oh, I meant to say it's five minutes past eleven.

Huan **'I: 'antṣ 'eḍa o cem cipkanam gamai-hemako-ceḍ. T o 'amhu has ñ-a: g ñ-malioñga.**
Oh no, and I was supposed to go to work at eleven. My boss is liable to say bad things about me.

EXERCISES

A. Use all of the new nouns in some original Papago sentences.

B. Use all of the possible forms of the *because* word in some Papago sentences.

C. Make up three original questions and answers referring to the time on a clock.

LESSON 25

Going to the Store and to the Doctor

VOCABULARY

NOUNS

Singular	*Plural*
na:kaj his, her, its ear	**na:nkaj** his, her, its ears
melimdam traveler, person traveling to a particular place	**wo:po'imdam** travelers, persons traveling to a particular place
we:s ha'icu everything	—

VERBS

cecega *perf.* checked	**cecega** checked
cekeidag being able to hear	**cekeidag** being able to hear
'eñga having to	**'eñga** having to
'e-ju: doing	**'e-wua** doing
'i-bei *perf.* brought, took	**'i-ui** brought, took
kaij saying	**kaij** saying
ko'ito *perf.* ate (it) up	**ko'ito** ate (it) up
s-himim desiring to go	**s-hihimim** desiring to go
s-'oidamk desiring to go with, follow	**s-oidamk** desiring to go with, follow

OTHER EXPRESSIONS

cuhug at night, last night
'e-elid he, she, it thinks
mu'ic many

NOTE: In the dialog which follows, some of the forms of the aux appear with ṣ attached to them as a suffix. This form of the aux indicates that the situation described in the sentences is something which is not witnessed by the speaker, but is simply being reported by the speaker. These auxiliary forms, then, indicate something like "reportedly" or "apparently."

It is possible to attach the ṣ to both the imperfective and the perfective forms of the aux. For example:

Hegai 'aṣ cipkan. He (she) is/was apparently working.

'A:pim 'amṣ 'am o hihi. You (*pl.*) are apparently going to go there.

'A:cim 'attṣ o cickp. We are apparently going to work.

'A:pim 'amtṣ o cicwi. You (*pl.*) are apparently going to play.

Notice that the third person singular form (*sg. and pl.*) changes from **'o** to **'aṣ** in this "reported" form.

DIALOG

Klisti:na **Natṣ 'am o hi: g Husi tianda wui?**
Did Joe say he will go to the store?

Mali:ya **Ta:pĭ. Hascu 'a:gĭ?**
I don't know. Why?

Klisti:na **Ṣag wepo mo b kaij g ñ-je'e maṣ hab kaij g Husi matṣ 'am o s-himim tianda wui.**
I think that my mother said that Joe said that he might go to the store today.

Mali:ya **Naṣ 'eḍa cem s-oidamk?**
Does she want to go with him?

Klisti:na **Ha'u, naṣpi mu'i ha'icu taicu 'ab tianda 'amjeḍ . . . we:s ha'icu 'atṣ ko'ito hegam cuhug.**
Yes, because apparently she needs many things from the store . . . everything was eaten up by them last night.

Mali:ya **'A: ha'u, 'añ ba ñeid mo mu'ic g mamgina 'am m-ki: 'am cuhug.**
Oh yes, I noticed that there were many cars at your house last night.

Klisti:na **Ha'u, hegam ñ-wepnag 'atṣ 'am wo'i; Cuk Ṣon 'amjeḍ 'aṣ wo:po'o c 'aṣ 'am Phoenix wui ḍ wo:poimdam.**
Yes, apparently my brothers and sisters arrived; they were coming from Tucson and were on their way to Phoenix.

Mali:ya **Tṣ has o 'e-ju: 'am Phoenix t-am?**
What are they going to do in Phoenix?

Klisti:na **'Ali 'atṣ 'am o 'i-bei makia wui natṣpi 'eñiga o cecega g makia g na:nkaj. B 'o 'a:gĭ maṣ pi 'ap ha'icu ka: g 'ali.**
Apparently they are taking the child to the doctor because the doctor has to check the child's ears. It is said that the child can't hear very well.

Mali:ya **Ge pi 'al cekeidag?**
The poor thing is slightly deaf?

Klisti:na **Ha'u, b 'aṣ 'e-elid g je'ej. Pegi, nappi o ṣa ñei g Husi k b o a: mo s-oidam g ñ-je'e.**
Yes, that is what the mother thinks. Well, if you should see Joe tell him that my mother wants to go with him.

Mali:ya **Pegi 'oig.**
Okay.

EXERCISES

A. Use each of the new nouns in an original Papago sentence.

B. Use each of the new verbs and phrases in an original Papago sentence.

C. Write five original Papago sentences using the *reported* marker ṣ on the auxiliary.

PART IV
Supplementary Material

Abbreviations and Symbols

ABBREVIATIONS

AUX	auxiliary (verb)
DET	determiner (*the, a*)
D.O.	direct object
IMPERF.	imperfective verb
I.O.	indirect object
N.	noun
NEG	negative
perf.	perfective verb
pl.	plural
sg.	singular
v.	verb

SYMBOLS

*	grammatically incorrect
ʾ	glottal stop
˘	short vowel
:	long vowel
~	tilde
ṣ	retroflex s
ḍ	retroflex d
ŋ	engwa

Summary of Grammatical Elements

AFFIXES AND SUFFIXES

AFFIXES TO VERBS

-ad *future imperfective*
'i- *directional imperative*
-iñ *imperative*
-kuḍ *turns verbs into instrumental nouns*

SUFFIXES TO NOUNS

-ga *possession marker for alienably possessed nouns*
-mad *turns nouns into verbs*
-pig *turns nouns into verbs*

QUESTION WORDS

PRE-AUXILIARY FORM	POST-AUXILIARY FORM
ba: where	**hebai** where
do: who, whom	**heḍai** who, whom
ṣa: what (*abstract*)	**has** what (*abstract*)
ṣa:cu what (*concrete*)	**hascu** what (*concrete*)

he'ekio how many

PARTICLES AND SMALL ELEMENTS

g the, a (*determiner*)
ki than (*used in comparatives*)
m *subordinate clause marker*
n *question marker*
o *future marker*
pi not (*negative*)
wuḍ/ḍ *copula, linking word*

PRONOUNS

INDEPENDENT PRONOUNS (SUBJECTS & DIRECT OBJECTS)

	Singular			*Plural*		
	LONG FORM	SHORT FORM		LONG FORM	SHORT FORM	
1st per.	**'a:ñi**	**'a:ñ**	I, me	**'a:cim**	**'a:c**	we, us
2nd per.	**'a:pi**	**'a:p**	you	**'a:pim**	**'a:p**	you
3rd per.	**hegai**	**heg**	he, she, it, that; him, her, it, that	**hegam**	**heg**	they, those; them, those

DIRECT AND INDIRECT OBJECT PREFIXES

	Singular		*Plural*	
1st person	**ñ-**	me	**t-**	us
2nd person	**m-**	you	**'em-**	you
3rd person	—	him, her, it; that	**ha-**	them; those

POSSESSIVE AFFIXES

	Singular		*Plural*	
1st person	**ñ-**	my	**t-**	our
2nd person	**m-**	your	**'em-**	your
3rd person	**-ij, -j**	his, her, its	**ha-**	their

POSTPOSITIONAL OBJECT PREFIXES

	Singular		*Plural*	
1st person	**ñ-**	me	**t-**	us
2nd person	**m-**	your	**'em-**	you
3rd person	**ha-**	him, her, it; that	**ha-**	them; those

REFLEXIVE PREFIXES

	Singular		*Plural*	
1st person	**ñ-**	myself	**t-**	ourselves
2nd person	**'e-**	yourself	**'e-**	yourselves
3rd person	**'e-**	himself, herself, itself	**'e-**	themselves

AUXILIARY FORMS

	Singular			*Plural*		
	LONG FORM	SHORT FORM		LONG FORM	SHORT FORM	
			IMPERFECTIVE AUXILIARY			
1st person	**'añ**	**ñ**	am/was	**'ac**	**c**	are/were
2nd person	**'ap**	**p**	are/were	**'am**	**m**	are/were
3rd person	**'o**	**'o**	is/was	**'o**	**'o**	are/were
			PERFECTIVE AUXILIARY*			
1st person	**'ant**	**nt**		**'att**	**tt**	
2nd person	**'apt**	**pt**		**'amt**	**mt**	
3rd person	**'at**	**t**		**'at**	**t**	
			SPECIAL IMPERFECTIVE AUXILIARY FORMS (in Conjoined Sentences and Interrogative Sentences)			
1st person	**kuñ**	**ñ**	am/was	**kuc**	**c**	are/were
2nd person	**kup**	**p**	are/were	**kum**	**m**	are/were
3rd person	—	**k**	is/was	—	**k**	are/were

*Perfective auxiliary does not translate.

Glossary
Papago to English

The Papago to English glossary is listed in standard alphabetical order, which is not affected by glottal stops or long vowels. Within this system ḍ follows d, ñ follows n, ŋ follows ñ, and ṣ follows s. Nouns and verbs are identified as such; both singular and plural forms are shown. Verbs are listed according to their singular imperfective forms, with the plural imperfective and singular and plural perfective forms following, if appropriate. If the plural of a noun or verb is so different from the singular that it would be difficult to locate, the plural is also listed as a separate entry.

A

'ab against, toward speaker, at, on

'ac, c are/were

'a:cim, 'a:c we, us *pl.*

-ad *future imperfective marker*

a:gid, 'a:g, 'a:gĭ *v.,* telling, saying *sg. and pl.;* **b 'o 'e-a:gĭ** it is said

'a'i each other

'ajij (being) thin, narrow; **'a'ajij** *pl.; no perf.*

'Akimel 'O'odham *n.* Pima person *sg. and pl.*

'ali *n.* child, baby; **'a'al** *pl.*

'alidag *n.* child of a man; **'a'alidag** *pl.*

'am, m are/were

'am away from speaker

'am here

'amai over there (*in front of speaker*), right there

'amhu over there, there

'amt, mt *perf. aux, 2nd person pl.*

'an next to speaker

'anai over there (*next to speaker*), right here (*next to*)

'ant, nt *perf. aux, 1st person sg.*

'añ, ñ am/was

'a:ñi, 'a:ñ I, me

'ap, p are/were

'a:pi, 'a:p you *sg.*

'a:pim, 'a:p you *pl.*

apt, pt *perf. aux, 2nd person sg.*

'asugal *n.* sugar; *sg. and pl.*

'aṣ just

'at, t *perf. aux, 3rd person sg. and pl.*

'att, tt, *perf. aux, 1st person pl.*

'auppa *n.* tree, cottonwood; **'a'auppa** *pl.*

B

ba: where *pre-aux form*

ba'a *v.* swallowing *sg. and pl.;* **ba:** *sg. and pl. perf.*

ba:b *n.* grandfather on mother's side; **ba:bab** *pl.*

ba:bas *n.* potato *sg. and pl.*

ba'ic in front of (a person); *see also* **ba:ṣo**

ba'ic 'i more *followed by* **ki** (than) *in comparative sentences*

ban *n.* coyote; **ba:ban** *pl.*

ba:ñimad *v.* crawling; **ba:bañimad** *pl; no perf.*

ba:ṣo in front of (a thing)

beihĭ *v., perf.* got, purchased (*for someone*); **'u'i** *pl. perf.*

bei *v., perf.* got, purchased (*for oneself*); **'ui** *pl.*

bidṣ *v., perf.* got muddy, dirty *sg. and pl.*

bisc *v.* sneezing *sg. and pl., sg. and pl. perf.*

bit *n.* dirt, clog of mud *sg. and pl.*

b 'o 'e-a:gĭ it is/was said

b 'o 'e-elid he thinks

b 'o kaij g Huan John said

bo:l *n.* ball; **bobol** *pl.*

b 'o ñ-a:gid he told me

C

c and

ca:ŋgo *n.* monkey; **cacaŋgo** *pl.*

ceḍ in, inside

ce'ewid *v.* covering *sg. and pl.*; **ce'ewi** *sg. and pl. perf.*

ce'ewidakuḍ, ce'ewikuḍ *n.* instrument used to cover with, blanket *sg. and pl.*

ceggia *v.* fighting *sg. imperf. and perf.*; **ceceggia** *pl. imperf. and perf.*

cehia *n.* young girl; **cecia** *pl.*

cei *v., perf.* said *sg. and pl.*

celkon *v.* scraping; **cecelkon** *pl.;* **celko** *sg. perf.;* **cecelko** *pl. perf.*

celpig *v.* scraping off, removing by scraping; **cecelpig** *pl.*; **celpĭ** *sg. perf.;* **cecelpĭ** *pl. perf.*

cemaj small; **ce'ecmaj** *pl.*

cem hekid always

cendad *v.* kissing *sg. imperf. and perf.;* **cecendad** *pl. imperf. and perf.*

ceoj *n.* boy, man; **cecoj** *pl.*

ceposid *v.* branding; **cecposid** *pl.;* **cepos** *sg. perf.;* **cecpos** *pl. perf.*

cewaj (being) tall, long; **ce'ecwaj** *pl.*

cicwi *v.* playing *sg. and pl., sg. and pl. perf.*

cicwikuḍ *n.* instrument to play with, toy; *sg. and pl.*

cihil *n.* scissors *sg. and pl.*

Ci:no *n.* Oriental person; **Cicno** *pl.*

ciñ, ceñ *n.* mouth; **ci:ciñ, ce:ceñ** *pl.*

cipkan *v.* working; **cicpkan** *pl.;* **cipk** *sg. perf.;* **cicpk** *pl. perf.*

cucul *n.* chicken *sg. and pl.*

cu:dp six

cu:dpo six times, the sixties

cu:hug, cu:kug *n.* meat *sg. and pl.*

cu'i *n.* flour *no pl.*

cu'imad *v.* adding flour to something, flouring; *sg. and pl., sg. and pl. perf.*

Cuk Ṣon Tucson

cu:wĭ *n.* jackrabbit *sg. and pl.*

D

ḍ *copular, linking word (short form)*

da'a *v.* flying, jumping; **ñe:ñe'e** *pl.;* **da:** *sg. perf.;* **ñe:ñ** *pl. perf.*

da:d *n.* senior aunt on mother's side; **da:da'a** *pl.*

dada *v., perf.* arrived *pl.*

dagkon *v.* wiping, drying; **dadgkon** *pl.;* **dagko** *sg. perf.;* **dadagko** *pl. perf.*

dahă *v.* sitting; **daḍhă** *pl.;* **dahiwa** *sg. perf.;* **dadhiwua** *pl. perf.*

dai *v., perf.* set (*object*) down; **dadṣ** *pl.*

daikuḍ *n.* chair; **dadaikuḍ** *pl.*

da:k *n.* nose; **da:dk** *pl.*

da:m on top of, over, above

do: who, whom *pre-aux form*

do'ag *n.* mountain; **dodo'ag** *pl.*

E

'e- yourself; yourselves; himself, herself, itself; themselves

'eḍa, 'eḍ inside, in

'eḍa *n.* entrails, insides; *no pl.*

'eḍapig *v.* gutting; **'e'eḍapig** *pl.;* **'eḍapĭ** *sg. perf.;* **'e'eḍapĭ** *pl. perf.*

'e:'eḍ *n.* blood; *no pl.*

'e'eñga *n.* item of clothing; *sg. and pl.*

'elid *v.* thinking *sg. and pl.*

'elidag *n.* hide, skin, peel; **'e'elidag** *pl.*

'elkon *v.* skinning; **'e'elkon** *pl.;* **elko** *sg. perf.;* **'e'elko** *pl. perf.*

elpig *v.* peeling; **'e'elpig** *pl.;* **'elpi** *sg. perf.;* **'e'elpi** *pl. perf.*

'em- you, your

'eñga *v.* owning *sg. and pl.*

'eñga own

'eñigadad *v.* dressing *sg., imperf. and perf.;* **'e'eñigadad** *pl., imperf. and perf.*

'ep again

'e:p another

'eṣ *n.* chin; **'e'eṣ** *pl.*

G

g the, a

-ga *possession marker*

ga'a *v.* roasting *sg. and pl.;* **gai** *sg. and pl. perf.*

gaḍhu, gḍhu over there (*out of sight of speaker*)

gahu, ghu over there (*in sight of speaker*)

ga'ikuḍ *n.* instrument to roast with, grill; **gaga'ikuḍ** *pl.*

gamai- *prefix added to one through nine for the teens*

gamai-gi'ik fourteen

gamai-go:k twelve

gamai-hemako eleven

gamai-waik thirteen

ganhu, gnhu over there (*next to speaker*)

gaswua *v.* combing *sg. imperf. and perf.;* **gagswua** *pl. imperf. and perf.*

gaswuakuḍ, gaswuikuḍ *n.* instrument used to comb with, comb, brush; **gagswuakuḍ, gagswuikuḍ** *pl.*

ga:t *n.* gun, bow; **ga:gt** *pl.*

gatwid *v.* shooting; **gagtwid** *pl.;* **gatwi** *sg. perf.*; **gagtwi** *pl. perf.*

gatwidakuḍ, gatwikuḍ *n.* instrument used to shoot with, gun; **gagtwidakuḍ, gagtwikuḍ** *pl.*

ge'ej, ge'e *v.* (being) big; **ge'egḍaj, ge'egḍ** *pl.*

gegosid *v.* eating, feeding *sg. and pl.;* **gegos** *sg. and pl. perf.*

gei *v., perf.* fell; **ṣul** *pl.*

gigi'ik eight

gigi'ikko eight times, the eighties

gi'ik four

gi'ikko- four times, the forties

gi'ipig *v.* removing fat from animal carcass *sg. and pl.*; **gi'ipĭ** *sg. and pl. perf.*

gogs *n.* dog; **gogogs** *pl.*

go:k two

gokko- twice, two times, the twenties

golon *v.* raking *sg. and pl.;* **golo** *sg. and pl. perf.*

golonakuḍ *n.* instrument used to rake with, rake; **goglonakuḍ** *pl.*

H

ha- him, her, it; them; those; their

ha'a *n.* bottle, jar, pot; **haha'a** *pl.*

ha'asa *v., perf.* finished, completed *sg. and pl.*

hagpig *v.* removing leaves; **hahagpig** *pl.*

ha:hag *n.* leaf *sg. and pl.*

hahawa then

ha'icu *n.* something, thing *sg. and pl.*

haiwañ *n.* cow; **hahaiwañ** *pl.*

hajuñ *n.* cousin, relative; **hahajuñ** *pl.*

hakit *n.* junior uncle on father's side; **ha:kit** *pl.*

ha:l *n.* squash; **hahal** *pl.*

has what (*abstract*), *post-aux form*

hascu what (*concrete*), *post-aux form*

ha:ṣañ *n.* saguaro cactus; **hahaṣañ** *pl.*

ha'u yes

hebai where, *post-aux form*

heḍai who, whom *post-aux form*

he'eḍkad *v.* smiling; **hehe'eḍkad** *pl.;* **he'eḍka** *sg. perf.*; **hehe'eḍka** *pl. perf.*

he'ekio how many

hegai, heg he, she, it; that

hegam, heg they; those, them

hehem *v.* laughing *sg. and pl.;* **hehĕ** *sg. and pl. perf.*

hehwogij *v., perf.* cooled *sg. and pl.*

hekaj *v., perf.* used *sg. and pl.*

hekid when

he:lwuin *v.* sliding; **hehelwuin** *pl.;* **he:lwui** *sg. perf.;* **hehelwui** *pl. perf.*

hema a

hemajkam *n.* person; **hehemajkam** *pl.*

hemako one

hetasp five

hetaspo- five times, the fifties

heu'u, he'u yes

hewek *v.* smelling *sg. and pl., imperf. and perf.*

hewel *n.* wind *no pl.*

hidoḍ *n.* food, stew, pot of food; **hihidoḍ** *pl.*

hihidoḍ *v.* cooking *sg. and pl.;* **hihido** *sg. and pl. perf.*

hikck *v.* cutting; **hihikck** *pl.;* **hikc** *sg. perf.;* **hihikc** *pl. perf.*

him *v.* walking; **hihim** *pl.;* **hi:** *sg. perf.;* **hihi** *pl. perf.*

hi:nk *v.* barking, yelling; **hihink** *pl.;* **hi:n** *sg. perf.;* **hihin** *pl. perf.*

hi:wodag *n.* sore, scab; **hihwodag** *pl.*

hoa *n.* basket; **hoha** *pl.*

hodai *n.* rock; **hohodai** *pl.*

hu: *v., perf.* ate *sg. and pl.*

huasa'a, huhasa'a *n.* plate; **huhasaha'a** *pl.*

huawĭ *n.* deer; **huhuawĭ** *pl.*

hu:c, huc *n.* fingernail, claw; **huhuc** *pl.*

huḍ *v., perf.* came down; **huhuḍ** *pl.*

huḍ *n.* sunset *sg. and pl.*

hugidan beside, next to *no pl.*

huhu'id *v.* chasing *sg. and pl.;* **huhu'i** *sg. and pl. perf.*

hu:kajid *v.* warming *sg. and pl.;* **hu:kaj** *sg. and pl. perf.*

huki *v., perf.* scratched *sg. and pl.*

hukpig *v.* picking off, picking at with fingernail; **huhukpig** *pl.;* **hukpĭ** *sg. perf.;* **huhukpĭ** *pl. perf.*

hukṣan *v.* scratching; **huhukṣan** *pl.;* **hukṣa** *sg. perf.;* **huhukṣa** *pl. perf.*

humuk nine

humukko- nine times, the nineties

hu:ñ *n.* corn, ear of corn; **huhuñ** *pl.*

hu'ul *n.* grandmother on mother's side; **huhu'ul** *pl.*

I

'i here

'i- *directional imperative*

'ia here

'i:bhai *n.* prickly pear; **'i'ibhai** *pl.*

'i:bhĕ *v.* breathing *sg. and pl., imperf. and perf.*

i:da this; **'idam** *pl.*

'i:e *v.* drinking *sg. and pl.;* **'i:** *sg. and pl. perf.*

'i'ihog *v.* coughing *sg. and pl.;* **'i'iho** *sg. and pl. perf.*

-ij his, her, its

'i:ma, 'im back here (*in back of speaker*)

-iñ *imperative suffix*

'ipuḍ *n.* dress; **'i'ipuḍ** *pl.*

'ispul *n.* stirrup; **'i'ispul** *pl.*

'i:wuk, 'i:wagĭ *n.* wild spinach; greens *sg. and pl.*

'i:ya, 'ia, 'i here, right here

J

je'e *n.* mother; **je:j** *pl.*

je'es *n.* senior uncle on mother's side; **je:jes** *pl.*

je:k *v.* tasting

jekkaḍ outside

je:ñ *v.* smoking (a cigarette) *sg. and pl.;* **je:j** *sg. and pl. perf.*

jeweḍ *n.* land, dirt *sg. and pl.*

jeweḍmad *v.* getting dirty *sg. and pl., imperf. and perf.*

jisk *n.* junior aunt on mother's side; **jijsi** *pl.*

jiwa *v., perf.* arrived; **dada** *pl.*

ju: *v., perf.* did *sg. and pl.*

judum *n.* bear *sg. and pl.*

ju:k *v.* raining *no pl.;* **ju:** *perf.*

Ju:kam *n.* Mexican-American (*male*); **Jujkam** *pl.*

ju:kĭ *n.* rain *no pl.*

jukto *v., perf.* finished or stopped raining *no pl.*

K

k is/was; are/were

k, kc and

ka: *v.* hearing *sg. and pl., imperf. and perf.*

ka:c *v.* lying (*inanimate object*); **we:c** *pl.; no perf.*

kahio *n.* leg, thigh; **kakkio** *pl.*

kahon *n.* box; **kakhon** *pl.*

kaij *v.* saying *sg. and pl.;* **cei** *sg. and pl. perf.*

ka:k *n.* grandmother on father's side; **ka:ka'a** *pl.*

kalit *n.* wagon, car; **kaklit** *pl.*

ka:m *n.* cheek; **ka:kam** *pl.*

kamiṣ *n.* shirt; **kakmiṣ** *pl.*

kawhi *n.* coffee *sg. and pl.*

kawyu *n.* horse; **kakawyu** *pl.*

kc and

kegcid *v.* cleaning *sg. and pl.*

keickwa *v., perf.* kicked *sg. and pl.*

keihin *v.* kicking *sg. and pl.;* **keihi** *sg. and pl. perf.*

ke:k *v.* standing; **gegok** *pl.;* **kekiwa** *sg. perf.;* **gegokiwa** *pl. perf.*

ke:li *n.* old man; senior uncle on father's side; **kekel** *pl.*

ki than

ki: *v.* living *sg. and pl.*

ki: *n.* house, home; **ki:k, ki:kĭ** *pl.*

ko'a *v.* eating *sg. and pl.;* **hu:** *sg. and pl. perf.*

koi *v., perf.* died *pl.*

ko:ji *n.* pig; **kokji** *pl.*

ko:k *v., perf.* slept *pl.*

kokda *v.* killing *pl., imperf. and perf.*

ko'okol *n.* chile *sg. and pl.*

ko'okolmad *v.* to add chile to *sg. and pl., imperf. and perf.*

ko:ṣ *v.* sleeping; **ko:kṣ** *pl.;* **koi** *sg. perf.;* **ko:k** *pl. perf.*

kotoñ *n.* shirt; **koktoñ** *pl.*

kownal *n.* government official; **kokownal** *pl.*

ku'agĭ *n.* wood *no pl.*

ku:bs *n.* smoke, dust *no pl.*

ku:bsmad *v.* making smoky, causing dust *sg. and pl., imperf. and perf.*

kuc, c are/were

-kuḍ *turns verbs into instrumental nouns*

kuḍut *v.* bothering *sg. and pl.*

kui *n.* mesquite tree, tree; **kukui** *pl.*

kuint *v.* counting *sg., imperf. and perf.;* **kukuint** *pl., imperf. and perf.*

kuintakuḍ *n.* instrument used to count with, ruler, calculator; **kukuintakuḍ** *pl.*

kulañ *n.* medicine; **kuklañ** *pl.*

kulañmad *v.* making well, curing *sg. imperf. and perf.;* **kuklañmad** *pl. imperf. and perf.*

kum, m are/were

kuñ, ñ am/was

kup, p are/were

L

lial *n.* money *no pl.*

li:wa *n.* jacket, coat; **lilwa** *pl.*

lo:go (being) crazy; **lolgo** *pl.*

lu:lsi *n.* candy *sg. and pl.*

M

m *subordinate clause marker*

m- you, your *sg.*

ma: *v., perf.* gave *sg. and pl.*

-mad *turns nouns into verbs*

maḍ *n.* child (*of a woman*); **ma:maḍ** *pl.*

ma:gina *n.* car, vehicle; **mamagina** *pl.*

ma'ihi *v., perf.* hit (*someone or something*) with an object *sg. and pl.*

maistla *n.* teacher; **mamaistla** *pl.*

ma:k *v.* giving; **mamk** *pl.*

makai *n.* doctor; **mamakai** *pl.*

mansa:na *n.* apple *sg. and pl.*

maṣcamakuḍ *n.* school; **mamṣcamakuḍ** *pl.*

maṣcamdam *n.* student; **mamṣcamdam** *pl.*

meḍ *v.* running; **wo:po'o** *pl.*; **me:** *sg. perf.;* **wo:p** *pl. perf.*

mehĭ *n.* fire *sg. and pl.*

mei *v., perf.* burned *sg. and pl.*

mel *v., perf.* arrived; **wo'i** *pl.*

memḍa *v.* running repeatedly; **wopo'o** *pl.; no perf.*

mi:l one thousand

Milga:n *n.* Anglo person; **Mimilga:n** *pl.*

mi:sa *n.* table; **mimsa** *pl.*

mi:stol *n.* cat; **mimstol** *pl.*

mo'o *n.* hair *sg. and pl.*

mo'o *n.* head, head of hair; **mo:mĭ** *pl.*

mu: *v., perf.* died; **koi** *pl.*

mu'a *v.* killing; **kokda** *pl.*; **mua** *sg. perf.;* **kodka** *pl. perf.*

mu'akuḍ *n.* instrument to kill with, gun *sg. and pl.*

mul *v., perf.* broke; **'o:mĭ** *pl.*

mu:la *n.* mule; **mumla** *pl.*

mumku (being) sick *sg. and pl.*

mu:ñ *n.* bean, pot of cooked beans *sg. and pl.*

N

n *question marker*

na:d *v.* making a fire; **nanda** *pl.;* **nai** *sg. and pl. perf.*

na:dakuḍ *n.* stove; **nandakuḍ** *pl.*

na:k *n.* ear; **na:nk** *pl.*

nalaṣ *n.* orange *sg. and pl.*

naw *n.* prickly pear cactus *sg. and pl.*

nawaṣ *n.* pocket knife *sg. and pl.*

nawoj *n.* friend; **nanwoj** *pl.*

nolawt *v.* buying *sg. and pl., imperf. and perf.*

nolawtakuḍ *n.* instrument used to buy with or buy at, money, store *sg. and pl.*

nowĭ *n.* hand, arm; **no:nowĭ**, **no:nhoĭ** *pl.*

Ñ

ñ- me; my; myself

ñe'e *v.* singing; **ñeñe'e** *pl.;* **ñei** *sg. and pl. perf.*

ñeid *v.* seeing *sg. and pl.;* **ñei** *sg. and pl. perf.*

ñe:ñe'e *v.* jumping, flying *pl.;* **ñe:ñ** *pl. perf.*

ñeok *v.* speaking; **ñeñok** *pl.*

ñu:kud *v.* taking care of (*something/someone*) *sg. and pl., imperf. and perf.*

O

o *future marker*

'o is/was, are/were *imperf. aux., 3rd person sg. and pl.*

'o: *n.* back *sg. and pl.*

'o:bĭ *n.* non-Papago person; **'o'obĭ** *pl.*

'oḍpig *v.* removing sand; **'o'o ḍpig** *pl.;* **'oḍpĭ** *sg. perf.;* **'o'oḍpĭ** *pl. perf.*

'o:gĭ *n.* father; **'o'ogĭ** *pl.*

'oi *v., perf.* went with, followed, accompanied *sg. and pl.*

'oig go ahead (*used to give permission*)

'oil *n.* oil *sg. and pl.*

'oilmad *v.* adding oil to *sg. and pl., imperf. and perf.*

'oimeḍ *v.* walking around; **'oyopo** *pl.;* **'oime** *sg. and pl. perf.*

'oks *n.* old woman, old lady; **'o'oks** *pl.*

'oksga *n.* wife (*possessive construction*); **'o'oksga** *pl.*

'oksi *n.* senior aunt on father's side; **'o'oksi** *pl.*

'o:mĭ *v., perf.* broke *pl.*

'on *n.* salt *sg. and pl.*

'onmad *v.* adding salt to *sg., imperf. and perf.;* **'o'onmad** *pl., imperf. and perf.*

'onpig *v.* removing salt from; **'o'onpig** *pl.;* **'onpĭ** *sg. perf.;* **'o'opĭ** *pl. perf.*

'o'oḍ *n.* sand *sg. and pl.*

'O'odham *n.* person, Papago person *sg. and pl.*

'o'ohan *v.* writing, drawing *sg. and pl.;* **'o'oha** *sg. and pl. perf.*

'o'ohana *n.* book *sg. and pl.*

'o'ohanakuḍ *n.* instrument used to write with or to draw with, paper, pencil *sg. and pl.*

'oyopo *v.* walking around *pl.*

P

pa:do *n.* duck; **papdo** *pl.*

pa:l *n.* priest; **papal** *pl.*

pa:la *n.* shovel; **papla** *pl.*

palwu:m *n.* perfume *sg. and pl.*

pa:n *n.* bread, loaf of bread; **papan** *pl.*

pa:nt *v.* making bread *sg., imperf. and perf.;* **papant** *pl., imperf. and perf.*

pa:ntakuḍ *n.* instrument used to make bread, oven, pan; **papantakuḍ** *pl.*

pi not

pi'a no

-pig *turns nouns into verbs*

pi ha'icu nothing (*concrete*)

pi has nothing (*abstract*)

pi hebai nowhere

pi heḍai nobody

pikcult *v.* taking a picture, making a picture *sg., imperf. and perf.;* **pipikcult** *pl., imperf. and perf.*

pikcultakuḍ *n.* instrument used to take a picture, camera; **pipikcultakuḍ** *pl.*

pimiando *n.* pepper *sg. and pl.*

pisalt *v.* weighing *sg. and pl. imperf.;* **pisal** *sg. and pl. perf.*

pisaltakuḍ *n.* instrument used for weighing, scale; **pipsaltakuḍ** *pl.*

pla:njakuḍ *n.* instrument used for ironing with, iron *sg. and pl.*

potol *n.* bronc; **poptol** *pl.*

pualt *n.* door; **pupualt** *pl.*

S

s-añi:lmagĭ (being) blue *sg. and pl.*

s-ap (being) good, fine, (being) right *sg. and pl.*

s-ape (being) fine, all right *sg. and pl.*

s-ba:bigĭ (being) slow *sg. and pl.*

s-baga (being) angry; **s-babga** *pl.*

s-bi:dagĭ (being) dirty; **s-bibdagĭ** *pl.*

s-ce:dagĭ (being) green; **s-cecdagĭ** *pl.*

s-cuk (being) black; **s-cuck** *pl.*

S-Cukcu *n.* black person; **S-Cuckcu** *pl.*

s-da:pk (being) slippery; **s-dadpk** *pl.*

s-gakĭ (being) skinny; **s-gagkĭ** *pl.*

s-gi:g (being) fat; **s-gigk** *pl.*

s-he'ek (being) sour *sg. and pl.*

s-hemajima (being) friendly; **s-hehemajima** *pl.*

s-he:pĭ (being) cold *sg. and pl.*

s-he:pid (being) cold *sg. and pl.*

s-hewhogĭ (being) cool *sg. and pl.*

s-hottam quickly

s-hu:kĭ (being) warm *sg. and pl.*

si very, really

si'alim tomorrow

siant one hundred

sigal *n.* cigarette *sg. and pl.*

si'i *v.* sucking *sg. and pl.;* **si:** *sg. and pl. perf.*

si'ikuḍ *n.* instrument used for sucking, nipple, bottle; **sisi'ikuḍ** *pl.*

si:l *n.* saddle *sg. and pl.*

Sinaḍ *n.* Mexican-American, Mexican (*female*); **Sisnaḍ** *pl.*

s-i'owĭ (be) sweet, good-tasting *sg. and pl.*

siswui *n.* spit *no pl.*

siswuimad *v.* spitting on (*something/someone*) *sg. and pl., imperf. and perf.*

si:ṣp *v.* pinning, nailing; **sisiṣp** *pl.;* **si:ṣ** *sg. perf.;* **sisiṣ** *pl. perf.*

si:ṣpakuḍ *n.* instrument used to pin with, pin; **sisiṣpakuḍ** *pl.*

sitol *n.* honey, syrup *sg. and pl.*

sitolmad *v.* adding honey to *sg. and pl., imperf. and perf.*

siwĭ (being) sour, bitter *sg. and pl.*

s-ju:k (being) deep *sg. and pl.*

s-kaidag (being) loud *sg. and pl.*

s-kaidam loudly

s-kawi:magĭ (being) brown; **s-kakawi:magĭ** *pl.*

s-kawk (being) hard, dry; **s-kakawpk** *pl.*

s-ke:g (being) pretty, good-looking *sg. and pl.* (*used to refer to a person*)

s-ke:gaj (being) pretty, good-looking, good *sg. and pl.* (*applies to something other than a person*)

s-ko'ok (being) hot, spicy; painful *sg. and pl.*

s-ma:c *v.* knowing, understanding *sg. and pl.*

s-mohogĭ (being) itchy, scratchy; **s-momhogĭ** *pl.*

s-moik (being) soft; **s-momoik** *pl.*

s-mu'uk (being) sharp; **s-mu'umk** *pl.*

s-nakosig (being) noisy; **s-nankosig** *pl.*

s-nalaṣmagĭ (being) orange; **s-nanalaṣmagĭ** *pl.*

s-namkig (being) expensive; **s-nanamkig** *pl.*

s-oam (being) yellow; **s-o'oam** *pl.*

s-onk (being) salty; **s-o'onk** *pl.*

s-padma (being) lazy; **s-papdma** *pl.*

s-tohă (being) white; **s-to:ta** *pl.*

s-tonĭ (being) hot *sg. and pl.*

s-wagima (being) industrious; **s-wapagima** *pl.*

s-we:c (being) heavy; **s-wepc** *pl.*

s-wegĭ red; **s-wepegĭ** *pl.*

s-wihonig (being) messy; **s-wiphionig** *pl.*

s-wohocid *v.* believing *sg. and pl.;* **s-wohoc** *sg. and pl. perf.*

Ṣ

ṣa if

ṣa: what (*abstract*), *pre-auxiliary form*

ṣa:cu what (*concrete*), *pre-auxiliary form*

ṣa'i actually, really *no pl.*

ṣa'i *n.* grass, hay *sg. and pl.*

ṣaliwĭ *n.* pair of pants; **ṣaṣliwĭ** *pl.*

ṣa:mud *v.* shooing away, herding *sg. and pl., imperf. and perf.*

ṣawoñ *n.* soap *sg. and pl.*

ṣawoñmad *v.* adding soap to, soaping *sg. and pl., imperf. and perf.*

ṣa:yo *n.* radio; **ṣaṣyo** *pl.*

ṣoak *v.* crying; **soañ** *pl.;* **sosa** *sg. and pl. perf.*

ṣoiga *n.* pet, horse; **ṣoṣoiga** *pl.*

ṣonhin *v.* hitting *sg. and pl.;* **ṣonhi** *sg. and pl. perf.*

ṣonpig *v.* removing by hitting, chipping off *sg. and pl., imperf. and perf.*

ṣonwuin *v.* pounding, hitting *sg. and pl. imperf.;* **ṣonwui** *sg. and pl. perf.*

ṣonwuinakuḍ, ṣonwuikuḍ *n.* instrument used to pound with, hammer; **ṣoṣonwuinakuḍ, ṣoṣonwuikuḍ** *pl.*

ṣopolk (being) short; **ṣo'oṣpolk** *pl.*

ṣu:dagĭ *n.* water *no pl.*

ṣul *v.* *perf.* put down, place down (*plural objects*)

ṣu:ṣk *n.* shoe, pair of shoes *sg. and pl.*

T

t- us; our; ourselves

taḍ *n.* foot; **ta:taḍ** *pl.*

taicu *v.* wanting *sg. and pl.*

tako yesterday

ta:lko *n.* powder, talc *sg. and pl.*

ta:lkomad *v.* adding talc to, powdering *sg. and pl., imperf. and perf.*

tapial *n.* paper; **tatpial** *pl.*

taṣ *n.* sun *no pl.*

taṣga *n.* watch, clock *sg. and pl.*

ta:t *v., perf.* touched *sg. and pl.*

tatal *n.* junior uncle on mother's side; **tatal** *pl.*

ta:tṣ *v.* parting hair *sg. and pl., imperf. and perf.*

ta:tṣakuḍ *n.* instrument used to make a part with, comb *sg. and pl.*

tianda *n.* store; **titianda** *pl.*

tlo:gi *n.* truck; **tlolgi** *pl.*

to:bĭ *n.* rabbit, cottontail; **totobĭ** *pl.*

toḍk *v.* snoring *sg. and pl., imperf. and perf.*

Tohono 'O'odham *n.* Papago person *sg. and pl.*

to:lo *n.* bull; **totlo** *pl.*

to:n *n.* knee; **to:ton** *pl.*

to:nk *n.* hill; **totonk** *pl.*

towa *n.* turkey; **totwa** *pl.*

U

'u'ad *v., perf.* brought *sg. and pl.*

'u:gk *v.* (being) high; **'u'ugk** *pl.*

'u:hum *v.* back (*to where one came from*)

'ui *v., perf.* got, purchased (*for themselves*) *pl.*

'u'i *v., perf.* got, purchased (*for someone*) *pl.*

'ul *v., perf.* stuck out, extended; **'u'ul** *pl.*

'u:s *n.* wood, stick, board; **'u'us** *pl.*

'u'uhig *n.* bird *sg. and pl.*

'uwǐ *n.* woman; **'u'uwǐ** *pl.*

W

wacwi *v.* bathing, swimming *sg., imperf. and perf.;* **wapcwi** *pl., imperf. and perf.*

wa:ga *n.* dough *no pl.*

wai *v., perf.* called *sg. and pl.*

waid *v.* calling *sg. and pl.;* **wai** *sg. and pl. perf.*

waik three

waikko- three times, thrice, the thirties

wainom *n.* knife; **wapainom** *pl.*

wakial *n.* cowboy; **wapkial** *pl.*

wakon *v.* washing; **wapkon** *pl.;* **wako** *sg. perf.*; **wapko** *pl. perf.*

wakonakuḍ *n.* instrument used for washing, washing machine, basin, soap; **wapkonakuḍ** *pl.*

wamigǐ, wamigid *v.* get up; **wa:pamgǐ, wa:pamigid** *pl.*; **wam** *sg. perf.;* **wa:pam** *pl. perf.*

wapkona *n.* wash, laundry

wapkonakuḍ *n.* washing machine *sg. and pl.*

waṣai *n.* grass, hay *sg. and pl.*

waw *n.* rock, cliff *sg. and pl.*

we:big behind, in back of (*something*) *sg. and pl.*

wecij (being) young *sg. and pl.*

weco under, beneath; **wepco** *pl.*

wegid *v.* lighting up; **wepgid** *pl.;* **wegǐ** *sg. and pl. perf.*

we:hejeḍ for

we:m with

we:nag *n.* brother, sister; **wepnag** *pl.*

wenog while

westma:m ten

wewa'ak seven

wewa'akko- seven times, the seventies

wi:b *n.* milk *no pl.*

wisilo *n.* calf; **wipsilo** *pl.*

wo'i *v., perf.* arrived *pl.*

wo'ikuḍ *n.* bed; **wo:po'ikuḍ** *pl.*

wonam *n.* hat; **wopnam** *pl.*

wo'o *v.* lying down; **wo:p** *pl.;* **wo'iwa, woi** *sg. perf.;* **wo:po'iwa, woi** *pl. perf.*

wo:p *v., perf.* ran *pl.*

wopo *n.* fur *sg. and pl.*

wo:po'o *v.* running *pl.*

wopo'o *v.* running repeatedly *pl.*

wopopig *v.* removing fur (*from animal carcass*) *sg. and pl.;* **wopopĭ** *sg. and pl. perf.*

wosk *n.* grandfather on father's side; **wopsk** *pl.*

woson *v.* sweeping *sg. and pl.;* **woso** *sg. and pl. perf.*

wosonakuḍ, woskuḍ *n.* instrument used for sweeping, broom; **wopsonakuḍ, wopskuḍ** *pl.*

wowoit *n.* junior aunt on father's side; **wo:poit, wopowit** *pl.*

wu: *v., perf.* tied up *sg. and pl.*

wua *v.* doing *sg. and pl.;* **ju:** *sg. and pl. perf.*

wuḍ, ḍ *copular, linking word*

wu:ḍ *v.* tying up *sg. and pl.;* **wu:** *sg. and pl. perf.*

wuḍakuḍ *n.* instrument used for tying, rope, twine; **wupḍakuḍ** *pl.*

wuhĭ *n.* eye; **wu:pui** *pl.*

wuhioṣa *n.* face; **wuphioṣa** *pl.*

wui to, toward

wu:lo *n.* burro; **wuplo** *pl.*

wupḍa *v.* roping, tying *sg. and pl.;* **wu:** *sg. and pl. perf.*

wu:ṣ *v., perf.* got out, came out; **wuha** *pl.*

wu:ṣad *v.* taking out *sg. and pl.*

Glossary
English to Papago

The English to Papago glossary is in standard alphabetical order and carries only singular forms for nouns and verbs. If more information is needed, refer to the Papago-English glossary, where all forms are listed.

A

a **hema, g**

above **da:m**

actually **ṣa'i**

adding chile to **ko'okolmad**

adding flour to **cu'imad**

adding honey to **sitolmad**

adding oil to **'oilmad**

adding salt to **'onmad**

adding soap to **ṣawoñmad**

adding talc, powder to **ta:lkomad**

again **'ep**

against **'ab**

all right **s-ape**

always **cem hekid**

am/was **añ, ñ, kuñ**

and **c, k, kc**

Anglo person **Milga:n**

angry (being) **s-baga**

another **'e:p**

apple **mansa:na**

are/were **'am, 'o, c, m, p, k**

arm **nowǐ**

arrived **jiwa, mel**

at **'ab**

ate **hu:**

aunt. *See* junior aunt; senior aunt

away from speaker **'am**

B

baby **'ali**

back *n.* **'o:**

back **'u:hum** (*to where one came from*)

back here **'i:ma**

ball **bo:l**

barking **hi:nk**

basin **wakonakuḍ**

basket **hoa**

bathing **wacwi**

bean, pot of beans **mu:ñ**

bear **judum**

bed **wo'ikuḍ**

behind **we:big**

believing **s-wohocid**

beneath **weco**

beside **hugidan**

big **ge'ej**

bird **'u'uhig**

bitter **siwĭ**

black (being) **s-cuk**

black person **S-Cukcu**

blanket **ce'ewidakuḍ, ce'ewikuḍ**

blood **'e:'eḍ**

blue (being) **s-añi:lmagĭ**

board **'u:s**

book **'o'ohana**

bothering **kuḍut**

bottle **ha'a**

bow **ga:t, mu'akuḍ**

box **kahon**

boy **ceoj**

branding **ceposid**

bread **pa:n**

breathing **'i:bhĕ**

broke **mul**

bronco **potol**

broom **woskuḍ, wosonakuḍ**

brother, sister **we:nag**

brought **'u'ad**

brown **s-kawi:magĭ**

brush **gaswuakuḍ, gaswuikuḍ**

bull **to:lo**

burned **mei**

burro **wu:lo**

button **wotoñ**

buying **nolawt**

buzzard **ñuwĭ**

C

calf **wisilo**

called **wai**

calling **waid**

came down **huḍ**

came out **wu:ṣ**

camera **pikcultakuḍ**

candy **lu:lsi**

car **kalit, ma:gina**

cat **mi:stol**

chair **daikuḍ**

chasing **huhu'id**

cheek **ka:m**

chicken **cucul**

child **'ali**

child (*of man*) **'alidag**

child (*of woman*) **maḍ**

chile **ko'okol**

chin **'eṣ**

chipping **ṣonpig**

cigarette **sigal**

claw **hu:c, huc**

cleaning **kegcid**

cliff **waw**

clock **taṣga**

clog of dirt **bit**

clothing (item of) **'eñga**

coat **li:wa**

coffee **kawhi**

cold (being) **s-he:pid, s-hepĭ**

comb **gaswuakuḍ, gaswuikuḍ**

combing **gaswua**

cooking **hihidoḍ**

cool (being) **s-hewhogĭ**

cooled **hehwogij**

copular **wuḍ, ḍ**
corn **hu:ñ**
cotton **toki**
cottontail, rabbit **to:bĭ**
cottonwood **'auppa**
coughing **'i'ihog**
counting **kuint**
cousin **hajuñ**
covering **ce'ewid**
cow **haiwañ**
cowboy **wakial**
coyote **ban**
crawling **ba:ñimad**
crazy (being) **lo:go**
crying **ṣoak**
cutting **hikck**

D

deep (being) **s-ju:k**
deer **huawĭ**
devil **jiawul**
did **ju:**
died **mu:**
dirt, clog of dirt **bit**
dirt, land **jeweḍ**
dirty (being) **s-bi:dagĭ**
doctor **makai**
dog **gogs**
doing **wua**
door **pualt**
dough **wa:ga**
drawing **'o'ohan**
drawing implement, pencil **'o'ohanakuḍ**
dress **'ipuḍ**
dressing **'eñigadad**
drinking **'i:e**
dry, hard (being) **s-kawk**
drying **dagkon**
duck **pa:do**
dust **ku:bs**

E

each other **'a'i**
ear **na:k**
eating **ko'a, gegosid**
eight **gigi'ik**
eighties **gigi'ikko**
eleven **gamai-hemako**
entrails **'eḍa**
expensive (being) **s-namkig**
extend **'ul**
eye **wuhĭ**

F

face **wuhioṣa**
fat (being) **s-gi:g**
father **'o:gĭ**
feather **'a'an**
feeding **gegosid**
fell **gei**
fifties **hetaspo**
fighting **ceggia**
fine, good (being) **s-ape, s-ap**
fingernail **hu:c, huc**
finished **ha'asa**
finished raining **jukto**
fire *n.* **mehĭ**
fire, making a **na:d**
firewood **ku'agĭ**
five **hetasp**
five times; fifties **hetaspo**

flour **cu'i**

flouring, adding flour to **cu'imad**

flying **da'a**

followed **'oi**

food **hidoḍ**

foot **taḍ**

for **we:hejeḍ**

forties **gi'ikko**

four **gi'ik**

fourteen **gamai-gi'ik**

four times **gi'ikko**

friend **nawoj**

friendly (being) **s-hemajima**

front **ba:ṣo**

fur **wopo**

G

gave **ma:**

getting dirty **jeweḍmad**

getting muddy **bidṣ**

getting up **wamigĭ**

girl **cehia, 'uwĭ**

go ahead (*used to give permission*) **'oig**

good, fine (being) **s-ape, s-ap**

good-looking **s-ke:gaj**

good-tasting **s-i'owĭ**

got (*for oneself*) **bei**

got (*for someone*) **beihĭ**

got muddy **bidṣ**

got out, came out **wu:ṣ**

governor **kownal**

grandfather on father's side **wosk**

grandfather on mother's side **ba:b**

grandmother on father's side **ka:k**

grandmother on mother's side **hu'ul**

grass **ṣa'i, waṣai**

green (being) **s-ce:dagĭ**

greens, spinach **'i:wagĭ**

grill **ga'ikuḍ**

gun **ga:t, gatwidakuḍ, gatwikuḍ, mu'akuḍ**

gutting **'eḍapig**

H

hair **mo'o**

hammer **ṣonwuinakuḍ, ṣonwuikuḍ**

hand **nowĭ**

hard (being) **s-kawk**

hat **wonam**

hay **ṣa'i, waṣai**

he **hegai, heg**

head **mo'o**

hearing **ka:**

heavy (being) **s-we:c**

her **-ij, ha-**

herding **ṣa:mud**

here **'i:ya, 'i, 'ia, am**

herself **'e-**

he said **b 'o kaij**

he thinks **b 'o 'e-elid**

he told me **b 'o ñ-a:gid**

hide **'elidag**

high (being) **'u:gk**

hill **to:nk**

him **hegai, heg; ha-**

himself **'e-**

his **-ij, ha-**

hit (*with an object*) **ma'ihi**

hitting **ṣonhin, ṣonwuin**

home **ki:**

honey, syrup **sitol**

horn **'a'ag**

horse **kawyu**

hot, spicy, painful (being) **s-ko'ok**

hot (being), *temperature* **s-tonĭ**

house **ki:**

how many **he'ekio**

human being **hemajkam**

I

I, me **'a:ñi, 'añ**

if **ṣa**

in **'eḍa, ceḍ**

in back of **we:big**

industrious (being) **s-wagima**

infection **hi:wodag**

in front of **ba'ic; ba:ṣo**

inside **'eḍa, 'eḍ**

insides **'eḍa**

instrument for buying with or at; money, store **nolawtakuḍ**

instrument for combing; comb, hairbrush **gaswuakuḍ, gaswuikuḍ**

instrument for counting or measuring; ruler **kuintakuḍ**

instrument for covering; blanket **ce'ewidakuḍ, ce'ewikuḍ**

instrument to iron with; iron **pla:njakuḍ**

instrument to kill with, gun, bow **mu'akuḍ**

instrument to make bread, an oven; pan **pa:ntakuḍ**

instrument to make a part with; comb **ta:tṣakuḍ**

instrument to pin with; pin **si:ṣpakuḍ**

instrument to play with; toy **cicwikuḍ**

instrument to pound with; hammer **ṣonwuinakuḍ, ṣonwuikuḍ**

instrument to rake with; rake **golonakuḍ**

instrument to roast with; grill **ga'ikuḍ**

instrument to shoot with; gun **gatwidakuḍ, gatwikuḍ**

instrument for sucking; nipple **si'ikuḍ**

instrument to sweep with; broom **wosonakuḍ, woskuḍ**

instrument to take a picture with; camera **pikcultakuḍ**

instrument to tie with; rope **wuḍakuḍ**

instrument to wash with or in; basin, soap **wakonakuḍ**

instrument to weigh with; scale **pisaltakuḍ**

instrument to write or draw with; pencil, paper **'o'ohanakuḍ**

iron **pla:njakuḍ**

is/was **'o, k**

it **hegai, heg; ha-**

itchy (being) **s-mohogĭ**

item of clothing **'e'eñga**

it is said **b 'o 'e-a:gĭ**

its **-ij**

itself **'e-**

J

jacket **li:wa**

jackrabbit **cu:wĭ**

jar **ha'a**

John said **b 'o kaij g Huan**

jumped **da:**

junior aunt on father's side **wowoit**

junior aunt on mother's side **jisk**

junior uncle on father's side **hakit**

junior uncle on mother's side **tatal**

just **'aṣ**

K

kicked **keihi, keickwa**

kicking **keihin**

killed **mua**

killing **mu'a**

kissing **cendad**

knee **to:n**

knowing **s-ma:c**

L

land **jeweḍ**

laughing **hehem**

laundry, wash **wapkona**

lay down **wo'iwa, woi**

lazy (being) **s-padma**

leaf **ha:hag**

leg, thigh **kahio**

lemon **limo:n**

lighting up **wegid**

living **ki:**

lizard **hujuḍ**

long **cewaj**

loud (being) **s-kaidag**

loudly **s-kaidam**

lying (*object*) **ka:c**

lying down **wo'o**

M

making bread **pa:nt**

making dusty, causing dust **ku:bsmad**

making a fire **na:d**

making a picture **pikcult**

making well **kulañmad**

man **ceoj, ke:li**

me, I **'a:ñi, 'añ, ñ-**

meat **cu:hug, cu:kug**

medicine **kulañ**

mesquite **kui**

messy (being) **s-wihonig**

Mexican-American (female) **Si:naḍ**

Mexican-American (male) **Ju:kam**

milk **wi:b**

mine **'eñga**
money **lial, nolawtakuḍ**
monkey **ca:ŋgo**
more **ba'ic 'i**
mother **je'e**
mountain **do'ag**
mouth **ciñ, ceñ**
mud **bit**
mule **mu:la**
my, myself **ñ-**

N

narrow (being) **'ajij**
next to (*an object*) **hugidan**
next to (*speaker*) **'an**
nine **humuk**
nine times **humukko**
nipple **si'ikuḍ**
no **pi'a**
nobọdy **pi heḍai**
noisy (being) **s-nakosig**
non-Papago person **'o:bĭ**
nose **da:k**
not **pi**
nothing (*abstract*) **pi has**
nothing (*concrete*) **pi ha'icu**
nowhere **pi hebai**

O

official **kownal**
oil **'oil**
oiling **'oilmad**
old man **ke:li**
old woman, old lady **'oks**
on **'ab**
one **hemako**
one hundred **siant**
one thousand **mi:l**
on top of **da:m**
orange *n.* **nalaṣ**
orange (being) **s-nalaṣmagĭ**
Oriental person **Ci:no**
our, ourselves **t-**
outside **jekkaḍ**
oven **pa:ntakuḍ**
over there **'am, 'amhu, mhu**
over there (*in front of speaker*) **'amai**
over there (*in sight of speaker*) **gahu, ghu**
over there (*next to speaker*) **'anai, ganhu, gnhu**
over there (*out of sight of speaker*) **gaḍhu, gḍhu**
owning **'eñga**

P

painful (being) **s-ko'ok**
pan **pa:ntakuḍ**
pants, pair of pants **ṣaliwĭ**
Papago person **'O'odham, Tohono 'O'odham**
paper **'o'ohanakuḍ, tapial**
parting hair **ta:tṣ**
peel **'elidag**
peeling **'elpig**
pencil **'o'ohanakuḍ**
pepper **pimiando**
perfume **palwu:m**
person **hemajkam; 'O'odham**
pet **ṣoiga**
picking off **hukpig**

pig **ko:ji**
Pima **'Akimel 'O'odham**
pin **si:ṣpakuḍ**
pinned down **si:ṣ**
pinning **si:ṣp**
plate **huasa'a**
playing **cicwi**
pocket knife **nawaṣ**
pot **ha'a**
potato **ba:bas**
pot of food **hidoḍ**
pounding **ṣonwuin**
powder **ta:lko**
powdering **ta:lkomad**
pretty (being) **s-ke:gaj, s-ke:g**
prickly pear **'i:bhai, naw**
priest **pa:l**
purchased (*for oneself*) **bei**
put down *(plural objects)* **ṣul**

Q

quickly **s-hottam**

R

rabbit **to:bĭ**
radio **ṣa:yo**
rain **ju:kĭ**
rained **ju:**
raining **ju:k**
rake **golonakuḍ**
raking **golon**
really, very **si**
red **s-wegĭ**
relative **hajuñ**
removing by hitting **ṣonpig**
removing by scraping **celpig**
removing fat from animal carcass **gi'ipig**
removing fur **wopopig**
removing leaves **hagpig**
removing salt **'onpig**
removing sand **'oḍpig**
right here **'i:ya**
right there (*in front of speaker*) **'amai**
roasting **ga'a**
rock **hodai, waw**
rope **wuḍakuḍ**
roping **wupḍa**
ruler **kuintakuḍ**
running **meḍ**
running repeatedly **memḍa**

S

saddle **si:l**
saguaro **ha:ṣañ**
said **cei**
salt **'on**
salting **'onmad**
salty (being) **s-onk**
sand **'o'oḍ**
saying **kaij**
scab **hi:wodag**
scale **pisaltakuḍ**
school **maṣcamakuḍ**
scissors **cihil**
scraping **celkon**
scraping off **celpig**
scratched **huki**
scratching **hukṣan**
scratchy (being) s-mohogĭ
seeing **ñeid**

senior aunt on father's side **'oksi**
senior aunt on mother's side **da:d**
senior uncle on father's side **ke:li**
senior uncle on mother's side **je'es**
set (object) down **dai**
seven **wewa'ak**
seventies **wewa'akko**
sharp (being) **s-mu'uk**
she **hegai, heg**
shirt **kamiṣ, kotoñ**
shoes **ṣu:ṣk**
shooting **gatwid**
short (being) **ṣopolk**
shovel **pa:la**
sick (being) **mumku**
singing **ñe'e**
sister, brother **we:nag**
sitting **dahă**
six **cu:dp**
six times, sixties **cu:dpo**
skin **'elidag**
skinning **'elkon**
skinny (being) **s-gakĭ**
sleeping **ko:ṣ**
slept **koi**
sliding **he:lwuin**
slippery (being) **s-da:pk**
slow (being) **s-ba:bigĭ**
small **cemaj**
smelling **hewek**
smiling **he'eḍkad**
smoke *n.* **ku:bs**
smoking (a cigarette) **je:ñ**
sneezing **bisc**
snoring **toḍk**
soap **ṣawoñ, wakonakuḍ**
soaping **ṣawoñmad**
soft (being) **s-moik**
something **ha'icu**
sore **hi:wodag**
sour (being) **s-he'ek**
speaking **ñeok**
spicy (being) **s-ko'ok**
spit *n.* **siswui**
spitting on **siswuimad**
squash *n.* **ha:l**
standing **ke:k**
stew **hidoḍ**
stick *n.* **'u:s**
stirrup **'ispul**
stopped raining **jukto**
store *n.* **tianda, nolawtakuḍ**
stove **na:dakuḍ**
stuck out **'ul**
student **maṣcamdam**
sucking **si'i**
sugar **'asugal**
sun **taṣ**
sunset **huḍ**
swallowing **ba'a**
sweeping **woson**
sweet (being) **s-i'owĭ**
swimming **wacwi**
syrup, honey **sitol**

T

table **mi:sa**

taking a picture, making a picture **pikcult**

taking care of **ñu:kud**

taking out **wu:ṣad**

talc **ta:lko**

talking **ñeok**

tall (being) **cewaj**

tasting **je:k**

teacher **maistla**

telling **'a:g, 'a:gĭ, a:gid**

ten **westma:m**

than **ki**

that **hegai, heg; ha-**

the **g**

their **ha-**

them **hegam, heg**

themselves **'e-**

then **hahawa**

these **'idam**

they **hegam**

thigh, leg **kahio**

thin (being) **'ajij**

thing **ha'icu**

thinking **'elid**

thirteen **gamai-waik**

this **'i:da**

those **hegam, heg; ha-**

three **waik**

three times, thrice, thirties **waikko-**

tied up **wu:**

to, toward **wui**

tomorrow **si'alim**

touched **ta:t**

toward **wui**

toward speaker **'ab**

toy **cicwikuḍ**

tree **'auppa, kui**

truck **tlo:gi**

Tucson **Cuk Ṣon**

turkey **towa**

twelve **gamai-go:k**

twice **gokko**

two **go:k**

tying, roping **wupḍa**

tying up **wu:ḍ**

U

uncle. *See* junior uncle; senior uncle

under, beneath **weco**

understanding **s-ma:c**

us **t-; 'a:cim, 'a:c**

used **hekaj**

V

vehicle **ma:gina**

very **si**

W

wagon **kalit**

walking **him**

walking around **'oimeḍ**

wanting **taicu**

warm (being) **s-hu:kĭ**

warmed up **hu:kaj**

warming up **hu:kajid**

was/am **añ, ñ, kuñ**

wash, laundry **wapkona**

was/is **'o, k**

washing **wakon**

washing machine **wapkonakuḍ**
watch **taṣga**
water **ṣu:dagĭ**
we **'a:cim, 'ac**
weighing **pisalt**
went with **'oi**
were/are **'am, 'o, c, m, p, k**
what (*abstract*) **ṣa:, has**
what (*concrete*) **ṣa:cu, hascu**
where **ba:, hebai**
while **wenog**
white (being) **s-tohă**
who, whom **do:, heḍai**
wife **'oksga**
wild spinach **'i:wagĭ**
wind **hewel**
wiping, drying **dagkon**
with **we:m**
woman **'uwĭ**
wood **'u:s, ku'agĭ**
working **cipkan**
writing **o'ohan**
wrote **'o'oha**

Y

yelling, barking **hi:nk**
yellow (being) **s-oam**
yes **heu'u, he'u, ha'u**
yesterday **tako**
you (*sg.*) **'a:pi, 'a:p; m-**
you (*pl.*) **'apim, 'ap; 'em-**
young (being) **wecij**
young girl **cehia**
your (*sg.*) **m-**
your (*pl.*) **'em-**
yourself, yourselves **'e-**

Index

About the Author

Ofelia Zepeda is a member of the Tohono O'odham Nation. She was born and raised in Stanfield, Arizona, a rural cotton-farming community near the Tohono O'odham reservation. She holds a master's degree and a doctorate in linguistics from the University of Arizona, where she is a professor of linguistics. She has taught courses on the O'odham language, American Indian linguistics, American Indian language education, and creative writing for native speakers of Southwest Indian languages.

Dr. Zepeda is the author of a poetry book, *Ocean Power* (1995), and is a contributing author to several collections of Native American literature, including *The South Corner of Time* (1981), *Returning the Gift* (1994), and *Home Places* (1995). She is currently series editor of Sun Tracks, an American Indian literary series published by the University of Arizona Press.